TEN Arquitectos

TEN ARQUITECTOS

Enrique Norten
Bernardo Gómez-Pimienta

Texts by
Richard Ingersoll
Terence Riley
Michael Sorkin

The Monacelli Press

To my beloved children Sofía and Matías

EN

First published in the United States of America in 1998 by
The Monacelli Press, Inc.
10 East 92nd Street, New York, New York 10128.

Library of Congress Cataloging-in-Publication Data
TEN Arquitectos : Enrique Norten, Bernardo Gómez-Pimienta / texts by Richard
Ingersoll, Terence Riley, Michael Sorkin.
p.   cm.—(Work in progress)
Includes bibliographical references.
ISBN 1-885254-91-1   o
1. TEN Arquitectos (Firm). 2. Architecture, Modern—20th century—Mexico.
3. Functionalism (Architecture)—Influence. I. Ingersoll, Richard. II. Riley, Terence.
III. Sorkin, Michael, 1948– . IV. Title. V. Series: Work in progress (New York, N.Y.).
NA759.T35I54   1998
720'.92'2—dc21   98-7125

Printed in Hong Kong

Designed by Ricardo Salas, Frontespizio

Cover: National School of Theater
Page 2: Moda In-Casa
Page 4: Alliance Française
Pages 6–7: House LE

Photograph Credits
All photographs are by Luis Gordoa, with the exception of:
Michael Caldewood: page 24
Laura Cohen: page 34
Armando Hashimoto: page 110 (top)
Timothy Hursley: pages 111, 131, 135
Luis Montalvo: page 16 (first)
Tim Street Porter: pages 42, 47, 48, 49, 52, 53, 55, 57
David Resnikoff: page 43
Paul Zitrom: pages 16 (second), 46
Ursula Zülch: page 35

CONTENTS

PREFACE AND ACKNOWLEDGMENTS

Architecture demands a full-time commitment. In the last twenty years—I became an architect in 1978—there has not been for me one single day that was not dedicated somehow to architecture, either through study or research, through teaching, or through the actual practice of the profession; most frequently, the days absorb all of them simultaneously, with each activity addressing the others.

Although a book like this shows only the tangible events, highlights, and accomplishments of that everyday work—and only a few of those—it is really meant to celebrate the long and intense process that leads to the sparse instances of our career when we actually have the privilege of fulfilling the goal of architecture: the completion, in constructed form, of our daily work. In those brief glimpses, we live the moment of inhabitation as a culmination of our quotidian creative efforts.

I believe that our up-to-date body of work can be understood only by observing all of our projects, both built and unbuilt, and, through them, the effort we have dedicated to architecture over the years. Each one of these buildings informs the rest, complementing and contradicting each other at the same time. Although each may carry further some idea explored in one previous, every creation also addresses a new theme unique to its special and specific conditions. Each of these works may be seen as a destiny, but also as a departure for all to follow.

As it is impossible to include every one of our projects, I have selected a collection that I think represents the landmarks of our career. They are different in size, type, scale, program, and place, showing the various approaches and ideas with which we have confronted architecture. The selected work is organized chronologically with the goal of demonstrating the process through which we have journeyed. I have also included our most recent unbuilt projects, as well as those on which we are currently working, with the hope of indicating not only our freshest and most mature responses and ideas, but also of hinting at the future of our career.

Architecture is not an individual task; rather, it is the result of a complex team effort, with a large group of people coming together to complete a project. This book not only gives me a chance to analyze our work thus far and look into the future but it also offers me an opportunity to recognize and thank those who have joined us on this winding road, sharing with us their enthusiasm and expertise, their knowledge and their passion, and also supporting us and trusting our direction and beliefs.

First, I want to thank those who have made this book possible: Gianfranco Monacelli, Andrea Monfried, and Jen Bilik of The Monacelli Press have encouraged and motivated us to create this project. Thanks also to my friends Richard Ingersoll, Michael Sorkin, and Terence Riley, who offered to write texts for the book. To Cathy Ho, who helped me write the project texts. To Ricardo Salas, who patiently and beautifully designed the book, and to Luis Gordoa, who provided us with photographs of our work. And to the members of our team who worked in our office preparing the material for the book: Rosana Castañón, Catalina Aristizábal, Francisco Pardo, and Mark Seligson.

I am very grateful to all our consultants, to the contractors and workers who have participated in the projects and buildings, and also to every one of our team members, all those who have worked in our office and enriched our experience through the years.

All those people and institutions that have trusted us to do a project or build an edifice deserve a very special recognition. Good architecture can only be achieved by the partnership of a good architect and a good client; we have had the best. I only hope that we have met their expectations.

I am grateful to my partner, Bernardo Gómez-Pimienta, who has fought and endured with me through the bad times and with whom I have had the privilege of celebrating the good ones. And to his wife, Loredana Dall'Amico, for her support.

And last, but not least, I thank all of those who have made my life better: my parents, my friends, and, very specially, my beloved wife, Leticia, who has encouraged and motivated me every day since life brought us together.

The very best thing that has ever happened to me has been the birth of my children. They have helped me to understand the past, and have also given meaning to the future. They have showed me truth and beauty, they have brought light and energy to my life, they have given me new time and space. Thank you, my dearest Sofía and Matías.

ENRIQUE NORTEN
MEXICO CITY

11

FOREWORD

BY TERENCE RILEY

As one of North America's leading architects, Enrique Norten has established his presence in both the United States and Mexico as a practitioner, critic, and teacher. In his international outlook, Norten has broken from the pattern established by his fellow countryman Luis Barragán, whose masterly works constitute a profound exploration of national identity through architecture. Since its founding in Mexico City in 1985, TEN Arquitectos has explored the underlying currents surging through the international architectural community without abandoning strong local and cultural affinities. With his partner, Bernardo Gómez-Pimienta, who joined TEN in 1987, Norten has turned away from the masonry language that has dominated Mexican architecture for over one thousand years. TEN Arquitectos embraces a new language of light materials, complex forms, and daring techniques, creating easily recognizable associations with the work of contemporaries in Europe, Asia, and the United States.

In his essay "Six Memos for the Next Millenium" (1988), the Italian philosopher Italo Calvino identified three characteristics that define "lightness": first, to the highest degree possible, it is light; second, it is in motion; and third, it is a vector of information. TEN Arquitectos' preference for physically lightweight structural systems can be seen in a number of its Mexico City projects: the National School of Theater, in Churubusco (1993); the TELEVISA Services Building, in Chapultepec (1993); and the TELEVISA Dining Hall, in San Ángel (1992). In Calvino's terms, however, the lightness of Norten's architecture does not come from its relative weight but from the maximization of the concept of being light. This maximization and its relationship to structure is reflected in the Spanish language: a word for *light* (*luz*) is the same as the word for *span*. The enveloping structures of these buildings, simultaneously roof and facade, seem to hover with no apparent allegiance to gravity; in accordance with Calvino's view, they are not light like a feather but light like a bird.

Similarly, these structures embody motion; they seem to roll over the space within like benevolent cloud formations, folding the spaces upon themselves. Their elliptical sections amplify the sense of motion, providing no single static moment at which the structural forces would appear to rest. Furthermore, TEN Arquitectos projects consistently articulate the principal circulation systems—ramps, stairs, bridges—in such a way that the structures are seen as devices for motion and interaction; indeed, movement becomes a metaphor for interaction.

To define architecture as a vector of information would imply that architecture itself is not the source of information, but rather that architecture is capable of manifesting its environment. In this sense, the work of TEN Arquitectos is less concerned with issues of architectural style or personal expression and instead attempts to reflect the actual cultural circumstances that produced it. In the three projects mentioned earlier, interactive movement is not only experienced within the building but also between the architecture and the city beyond. The buildings' curvilinear forms not only define themselves within the urban context but also provide spatial continuity beyond their borders. Establishing a presence without resorting to the static monumentality of traditional forms, they allow for a fluidity of experience that remains the essence of urban experience.

Despite Norten's emergence as a transnational figure on the architectural scene, his work retains a distinct character influenced by the specific conditions of North America's most populous city. Like most urban centers that have experienced explosive growth during the twentieth century, Mexico City is marked by overwhelming complexities far beyond those that characterized any preindustrial city. The architecture of TEN Arquitectos exhibits a continuous series of refinements on that urban fabric with a simultaneous retention of a sense of gritty vitality. Avoiding the comfort of undecidedness, the work of TEN Arquitectos represents an urban strategy that sees the modern city not necessarily as coherent but as potentially legible. Most growing cities are developing in patterns similar to the sprawling expansion of Mexico City; with its reflection of these complex dynamics, Enrique Norten's architecture stands only to gain in its stature as an important source for study and insight.

Ten for TEN

by Michael Sorkin

Functionalism makes an ethic of precision, insists on an airtight fit between cause and effect, function and form. For true believers, style is simply a blind effect. While such materialist dogma may not cut much mustard nowadays, the structure of functionalism's argument remains the bedrock of architectural discourse: the form of a building must still, it seems, be justified by the method that produced it. However, the old priority accorded to a program of use has now been supplanted by a program of meaning. And that meaning can come from anywhere. Is modern architecture still possible in such a climate?

TEN's answer is surely a resounding "yes" to modernity. The architecture it makes subscribes squarely to the functionalist visual tradition, unabashed about the inspiration it draws from the technological muse and very refined in its relationship to both its sources and its materiality. TEN's project, however, is not formalistic. The firm has produced a body of work engaged with tasks of real civic consequence—workers housing, schools, public parks, museums, dining halls, markets—a truly enviable apparatus of contemporary community life, the program modernity always wished for itself.

All of TEN's projects completed to date are in Mexico, and one reason is suggested for this continuity: in Mexico, modernist forms retain the aura of progress—an optimism about the improvement of daily life—and the idea of progress still shines with an aspiration to democracy. For me, TEN's work, in its Mexican-ness, is strongly associated with an architectural tradition that is still unfolding, a modernism still directly connected to its origins rather than—as with so much practice today—simply conducting a reappropriation of images that have long outlived their original vitality. It is work without irony. Free of functionalism's austere yet hubristic account of itself, this architecture is free to pursue responsibility and beauty both.

Drawing on a tradition it clearly loves, TEN, although young, has already produced work of great maturity, focusing on an increasingly consistent set of visual, tectonic, and functional themes. Although it may be a little premature to codify TEN's overall character, these designs have clearly exhibited a strong and distinct signature, confidently entering the international conversation. It may not, therefore, be inappropriate to offer some notes—thematic clues, perhaps—for the magisterial study of TEN's oeuvre that will surely appear thirty years from now.

1. LONG FELLOWS

Love of length threads through TEN's work. Such attenuation distills; the mechanics of length is an enduring formal and conceptual preoccupation of modernity, suggesting speed, industrial apparatus, and, of course, the seriated division of film. For architects from Soria y Mata to Le Corbusier, the long building has been a grail, embodying the very idea of an alternative organization but still harboring the universalizing potential to girdle the Earth (if devolved now into the undreamed excesses of the strip). It's no coincidence that the stroll is the privileged medium for consuming the spaces of modernity: the semi-aimless, window-shopping, chance-driven drift through the metropolis (or the mall).

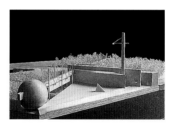

Above all, the long form contains the idea of circulation. At the extreme—Le Corbusier's Algiers project, for example—buildings become highways. Spines in the Children's Museum (1990, unbuilt) and the Los Olivos Park (1989, unbuilt) have a gentler mission, taking the form of land bridges, offering the simple pleasures of the stretch. At Tepito 2000 (1991, unbuilt), the promenade moves at the shopper's gait. At the Centro Automotriz (1991, unbuilt), linearity characterizes the service areas for cars. With some wit, the showrooms are contained in a tower, trapping and immobilizing the Mercedeses and Mazdas to emphasize their status as objects of consumption.

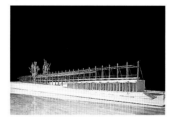

These linear elements, however, tend to be supported along their width, marking—asserting—the equal character of events within, deemphasizing end-on points of entry and departure, and expressing an apprpriate modesty about the literal necessity of the span. TEN's urbanism inserts fragments of this elongated movement—drawn from the histories of bridges and railways, airport finger-concourses and shopping malls—into the city of sprawl, rationalizing and socializing motion, if briefly.

2. SUSPENSION

Length produces the proclivity to suspend. There is no more dramatic means of foregrounding the medium of construction than suspension: hung structures celebrate lightness by, in effect, choosing to be supported from the sky. Never mind the fact that the weight is actually transferred down to the Earth; cables come from above. TEN's aesthetic derives much from this fundamentalist functionalism, from the spirituality of weightlessness, the ultimate architectural economy.

Those wires give a Malevichy look of crisscross dynamism and allow the roof section to be reduced to an ethereal thinness. At the TELEVISA Dining Hall (1992), at the Ola Azteca stadium and concert hall (1993, unbuilt), at the Moda In-Casa shop (1991)—indeed, in virtually all of TEN's work—there is an energizing pull of tension. Such construction focuses on its pieces, celebrating transparent assemblage, the fantasy of the kit of parts, modern architecture's analogue for nature. It also expresses a special attitude toward Mexico's eternal seismic crisis. These buildings are designed not to resist with manly Mayan stolidity but instead to bounce, flex, and ride it out.

3. TOWERS

TEN's buildings bristle with small towers and vertical addenda. Of course, this is the most traditional sort of compositional counterpoint: the Tepito 2000 market, the Centro Automotriz, the Museum of Sciences (1995, in progress), and, with the serendipitous adjacency of its broadcast mast, even the TELEVISA Services Building (1993) all have their secular steeples. TEN has a more-than-sneaking affection for those nineteenth-century boy toys, the bridges and battleships that form the primal muck of the functionalist aesthetic. But times have changed, and TEN's towers have thoroughly secular connotations, standing for communication plus anchoring plus marking plus observation plus a general tumescence.

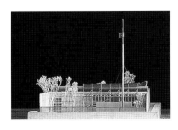

Other towers are more ad hoc. TEN's rooftops are fuzzy with electronic and other technical appurtenances, with antennae and satellite dishes and masts growing like crazy hair. One of the troubles for an architecture that keeps faith with the look of machinery is the machine's own transformation. As our technical achievements become increasingly immaterial (or at least invisible), the mimetic possibilities for stuff lag behind. This is why architecture's mimesis has shifted to theory. Because the machine no longer has a form, TEN seeks to grab some of this waning association between architecture and technology via the dematerialization of building mass through strategies of lightness ("less" is always the engineer's aesthetic) and through grafted icons—such as antennae—that stand for the transformative moment when a radio wave's effect becomes visible.

4. CANTING

On one side of TEN's first outdoor project, the Lighting Center (1988), a massive plane is canted out, becoming billboard, screen, lantern, and shadow-maker. The angled wall translates the found dynamism of the triangular plan into section. In many projects, TEN kickstarts its postconstructivist motor by inclining elements—in plan or section—away from the underlying orthogonality of primary forms and spaces, producing strobe shots of a frozen kinesis.

Recalling the primal vocabulary of modernity—manifest especially in the intoxicating form of the airport control tower, its glass faces angled away from the glare—TEN's canting is not about fashionable images of instability but about a purer form of composition and a more regular sense of motion. As noted, TEN loves to create tensile circumstances, and an outward lean is one of tension's primal scenes. At the TELEVISA Dining Hall, canted glazing parallels canted columns that hold the roof cables. A canted media wall—an elaborated, fluxing version of the wall at the Lighting Center—inclines to meet the rising path of escalators carrying workers to lunch. Along the path, lighting supports lean back as if resisting tension, reducing functional logics to matters of pure composition.

5. METAL

Metal and glass are the sine qua nons of the machine aesthetic. Enrique Norten has staked out a position as an unapologetic modernist distinguished by frank local inclinations; he writes about his search for a territory of locality in the context of a world culture. How, then, to integrate the metallic tradition with an architectural history that has never particularly embraced it, a rich modernism much more inclined toward density and shadow than toward lightness and reflectivity? Certainly, there is a modest oedipal aspect to this doing things differently, a reaction to a postbrutalist heaviness that has been popular in Mexico. But there is also an understanding that the mood has changed, that the global fantasy of progress is now fixed more on prosperity than on justice. TEN's modernity reflects its age, an age that has jets and cars and appliances for its symbols and aspirations.

But this is too reductive. TEN's taste is for a kind of materiality, a kind of surface, a kind of joinery, a kind of modulation of light, and, above all, for a kind of weightlessness that has long been a technical aspiration of a discipline that has gravity as its final frontier. TEN seeks artistically to embody global thinking in local action, keeping faith with both forms and materials. Engaging in a conversation that has participants in London, Los Angeles, New York, and Tokyo, TEN brings it all back home with lucid demonstrations not of modern architecture's indigenous origins but of its remarkable, persuasive suitability to site and program.

6. GRID

The grid is architecture's immemorial default, and it remains, both in mind and practice, the explicit organizer—though not the generator—of TEN's projects. Following the standard convention, TEN's working drawings are organized by a regular grid that is used not to defeat eccentricity but to locate it. Reading the work through this technical means of representation, I get a tremendous sense of reciprocity: TEN's irregularities always coexist with a permanent context of the regular. TEN's architecture, although never shy about eccentric moves, always feels orderly, consistent, and logical. The constant work of reconciliation with a mood of Cartesian repose informs—I think explicitly—this quality. In the most populous city in the world, one looks for a calm place.

Such a spirit of repose is the Zen of minimalism to which high modernism aspires both in its forms and in their relationship to content. TEN seeks to reconcile newer strategies

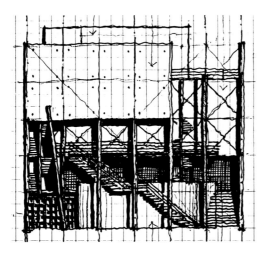

of ambiguity and inconsistency with this sense of simplicity. Here TEN truly engineers, embracing the idea that elegance lies in a clear and direct solution to a problem. TEN's talent, though, is to also defunctionalize the problem, to transpose this sensibility to problems of art, rigorously seeking rational solutions to questions with an irrational basis, to matters truly understood only by imagination and taste. The grid acts not as a backup for this quest but as an epistemology, a means by which any solution must ultimately be known. The fragments of this order, which appear throughout TEN's work, both acknowledge the real method of its creation and—at the next level—speak to the ways in which systematic self-observation can yield the site of language.

7. CURVES AND TUBES

There is something very disciplined about reserving your best curves for section. Although TEN was nearly there in the two TELEVISA sections and in the Santa Fe Pavilion (1994, unbuilt), the National School of Theater (1993) represents a breakthrough in confidence, sophistication, and the life of the curve. While the two rooftop projects push the arc through ninety degrees, the great roof at the theater school covers a more magnificent volume, sheltering not only so many tables and chairs but also a family of natural and built elements, a little theater of the world.

TEN's plan curves are also unusually suave. The predilection for length stretches these arcs toward flatness, yielding a characteristic and graceful plan form. The compression of these curves in the vertical, combined with their attenuation in the horizontal, produces the array of tubes that forms one of TEN's most typical formal aspirations: a space of continuous curvature. In straining toward this goal, TEN reconnects with the modernist project and its efforts to fashion a representation of the bent universe. For TEN, this abstract striving also yields great shade and an enlivened acoustic.

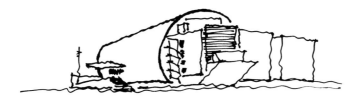

8. Layering

TEN makes thinness rich through lamination. I am thinking of House O (1990), hemmed into a small, difficult site by a hill and a busy road. Here the architects travel a long distance in a small space, from an aggressively public exterior to the quiet of an inner court. This transition is finessed by slipping the spaces of circulation behind a set of slightly skewed planes, by passing through one thin space after another, and by using courtyards both to catch the sun and to reinforce the sense of hemmed interiority.

This laminar style of deepening is visible even in TEN's early work. At the Alliance Française (1990), a thick screen wall begins a compact processional. As in House O, in the Alliance Française vertical circulation is positioned perpendicular to the axis of penetration and offers sidelong glances at its peelings-away. The screen itself is thick concrete and serves as a radically pared image of facade, not concealing but systematically revealing the metallic construction behind it. In the Workers Housing projects (1991), a similar device was employed on a long and deep site: a rectilinear masonry facade confronts the world while parallel bars of modest apartments tail off behind. The apartments—their own axes at right angles to the private walk, itself at right angles to the street—are screened by a light metal lamination that gives way to a masonry facade behind.

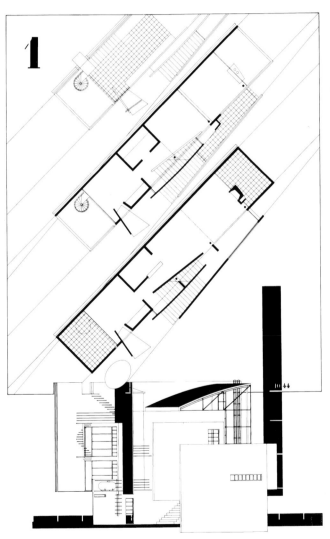

9. REPETITION

Repetition is the foundation of rhythm, whether it describes a dance or an assembly line. Here is another nub of modernity: the line between music and any organization of noises gets thinner and thinner—Philip Glass is the elevator music of the day. TEN (remember those long fellows) delights in the regular beat, arcing it just a bit in a kind of postmodern entasis, just enough to roll the eye. With its off-the-shelf panache, TEN understands that regular elements, whether of construction or of organization, are only the beginning, the means.

Like the syntax of the grid, the language of the bay and the module represents an organizational default that nonetheless holds the potential for recombination into more singular expressions. TEN accepts the quotidian orthodoxies of life, the idea that repeated patterns are what describe both an individual and a culture. It then tweaks these regularities through reorganization and embellishment to yield fresh forms of the familiar. For TEN, repetition is not a compulsion but a choice. And this is the best kind of architecture: no bludgeoning, just generous enlargements of horizon.

10. JOINTS

There is an art-historical bromide about the possibility of deriving the entire cathedral from the cross section of the pier. While the pier really only yields the vault, the idea of the summary part is crucial to modern views of the world, of evolution and the unified field: connection stands in for religion in the scientific age. As the most visible site of craft in the era of the machine, the joint is the godliest detail available, the detail that advertises a building's sense of fit. TEN makes great joints, filled with snug concision.

But let us finish with a bigger joint, a joint at the building scale. The TELEVISA Dining Hall is joined to a parking structure beneath, riding its roof, transforming it into an artificial ground. Much is made of this

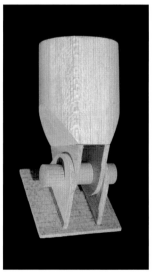

transition, emphasized by such elements as a very elegant ramp and twin escalators that pass through the screen of illusions, signaling the master illusion of a second ground. The nexus is a moment of non-coplanar sectional coexistence between the escalator tubes, the screen, the artificial grade, the natural grade, and the overhang of the kitchen roof. The joint works not so much as a moment of joinery but as an expression of convergence, and therein lies its elegance. By frankly letting things just come together, TEN produces—as always—what appears to be the only reasonable solution.

FESTINA LENTE
TEN ARQUITECTOS AND THE SWIFT SLOWNESS
OF MEXICO

BY RICHARD INGERSOLL

The imperial motto of Augustus Caesar, *festina lente*—make haste slowly—takes on new irony when one is caught in Mexico City traffic in a yellow Volkswagen taxi. Stalled on the grand boulevard Paseo de la Reforma, surrounded by barefoot children pawning Chiclets, one can see that the city embodies an involuntary paradox: Mexico City has both the quick pace of a metropolis and the exceedingly slow demeanor of an underdeveloped province. With a reported twenty-five million residents, the city is at once bursting at the seams as the world's largest conurbation while also retaining an uncanny villagelike feeling with its low-rise neighborhoods. Emerging Mexican architecture firms such as TEN Arquitectos that aspire to high technical standards and modern convenience cannot completely elude the retarding atmosphere that clings to the city with the persistence of the ash fallout from its two smoking volcanoes. An alluring slowness here envelops anything that moves fast, allowing the tortoise a clear advantage over the hare.

Enrique Norten, of mixed national origins and mixed education, is almost by default a transcultural architect, exhibiting in his designs a synthesis of slow (local) and fast (international) impulses. Although his father emigrated to Mexico with the German Jewish diaspora of the 1940s, Norten's cultural background remains predominantly Latin American. And while he received a second degree from Cornell University, his methods of working adhere more closely to Mexican traditions, allowing him an artistic status that is rarely granted to architects in the United States. Norten is, literally and intellectually, a creole, simultaneously belonging to two worlds without betraying either. Even if his work can superficially be associated with International High Tech through the assimilation of tension cables, structural glass, and complex curved shells, there is something in his architecture so particular to Mexico City in the siting, craftsmanship, formal solutions, and treatment of light that it should be immediately requalified as "Mex-Tech"—not unlike Mexican cuisine crossing the northern border, in the other direction, to become Tex-Mex.

Norten is the most adventurous and perspicacious practitioner among a new generation of so-called high-tech architects who are gradually gaining ascendancy in Mexico. As a generation, these younger architects have been influenced by the formal and ideological positions of two powerful trends that have made modern Mexican architecture among the most vital regionalist architectures in the world. These two trends are typified by the highly scenographic approach of Ricardo Legorreta, currently Mexico's most famous architect, known for his planar compositions with contrasting, vibrantly tinted "Mexican" colors, an inheritance from Luis Barragán; and the monumental, hollowed-out concrete volumes of Abraham Zabludovsky and Teodoro Gonzáles de León, in particular their majestic horizontal terraces, which convey the processional qualities of pre-Columbian cult centers.

The rejection by Norten and his cohorts of the explicit regionalism of these neo-Zapotec and neo-Aztec precedents was accompanied by a search for an appropriate design method rooted in the conditions of modern Mexican life. While the originality of TEN's structural solutions, the high quality of its details, and the sophistication of its typological investigations belong to an international quest of the sort celebrated at New York City's Museum of Modern Art in its "Light Technology" exhibition, in 1995, when seen in the context of Mexico City, TEN's buildings suggest a kind of stealthy contextualism. They respond more to the dirty realities of contemporary Mexican life in a crowded and polluted city than to the nostalgia for the colonial or pre-Columbian eras.

Norten's creole position, even though constructed within the peculiarities of Mexican patronage, offers a fresh answer to questions about the cultural function of architecture at the end of the twentieth century. The politics of identity, which tends to result in the employment of recognizable architectural style and character to gratify ethnic or regional stereotypes, regularly contradicts the desires for speed and flexibility in a modern way of life. In the postmodern creative milieu, which vacillates between a commitment to place and an obsession with time, the creole can be both of a place and in a time without compromising one to the other.

Mexico possesses one of the strongest samplings of modern-movement Latin American architecture from the 1930s and 1940s; further, technically sophisticated high-rise curtain-wall structures have been in continuous production in Mexico since the 1950s. The advent of the taste for high-tech details, however, has some connection to the presidential administration of Carlos Salinas de Gortari, from 1988 to 1994. Though in retrospect Salinas's government has become infamous for its corruption, it promoted a new openness to international development and technology in Mexico, as well as fostered an optimism that certain historic conditions of economic dependency could be reversed. Mexico, which has a substantial oil industry, joined an international financial community based on deregulation and flexible investment practices, a transition that culminated with the North American Free Trade Agreement (NAFTA). While parts of Mexico City, especially Santa Fe, the new business district, started to look like the edge settlements of Atlanta or Dallas, it is to TEN's credit that its work in these areas maintained a clear demonstration of professional integrity in the face of meretricious political and economic practices. This work provides a lesson in the commitment to craft, despite the dubious values of the times.

After working briefly for Zabludovsky and sharing a practice with Enrique Albin, Norten opened his own office in 1985. From the start, his independent work conceived of buildings as a series of independent layers held together with articulated joints. Norten's earliest work, boutiques and private houses, exhibits unconventional juxtapositions of materials and clever methods of assembly. Sheets of perforated aluminum fixed with tension cables, large panes of glass joined by steel suction brackets, veils of Teflon fabric held in place with steel purlins, and planes of steel-grill platforms are some of the initial material choices that have contributed to the overall feeling of transparency and buoyancy. The small hillside House O and the Alliance Française building (both 1990) are composed as vertical slices, stitched together with metallic structure and perforated at various intervals for a transparent effect. Although Norten's materials are often expensive and sometimes imported, each project obeys an underlying sense of economy in its practical circulation and layout, in its structural logic, and in its proper orientation to natural and urban conditions such that the expensive details seem to be good investments. If modern Mexican architecture is generally characterized by its strong monumental imagery and very poor details and construction, TEN has worked hard to reverse the priorities toward a genuine tectonic ethic. Norten seeks to design the most technically advanced building possible within the budget rather than denying the obvious attractions of modernity. In a country where mechanical devices regularly malfunction, it is truly a pleasure to find buildings that work.

The turning point in Norten's career came with the commission for a cafeteria addition (1992) to the suburban production site of TELEVISA, Mexico's largest private television conglomerate, which is run by one of the protagonists of Mexican deregulation, Emilio Azcárraga. Norten's design—an elliptical vault approached by skewed passarelles and fitted with an extruded billboard facade that serves as an exterior video screen—resulted in a spectacular image leading to widespread media exposure both locally and internationally. The success of the project secured three more commissions from the same client.

At the same moment in the early 1990s, Norten's office worked for the other end of the social scale. Its Workers Housing Brasil 75 (1991) is an infill structure that includes ground-level artisan spaces in Mexico City's historic center. While this project attracted less attention because of its modest program, it is equally important to the development of Norten's dynamic spatial language. Discreetly inserted next to the Church of Santa Catarina, the housing project demonstrates that, with careful selection of light-diffusing materials, including cheap metal cyclone fence, the interior patio can be elegantly reinvented without simulating historic models. The detached limestone facade, with its hollow slots, satisfies with ironic verve the stiff requirements for traditional scale and materials set by the architectural commission for the historic center. As a floating phantom, the facade proposes a poetic dialogue between the solid but seismically dangerous masonry techniques of the past and the light and translucent strategies of the future, as well as forcing a polemic with the idea of historic patrimony.

TEN's two major buildings, which to my mind fulfill the highest aspirations of Mexican architecture in the 1990s, are the TELEVISA Services Building (1993) and the National School of Theater (1993). Characterized by bulging metal shells, these buildings introduce a sublime formal novelty into the urban fabric as previously seen only in Paris and Tokyo. These tortoiselike agents of *festina lente* are strangely familiar. In essence they are like metal industrial sheds found all over Mexico City; in this case, they have been blown into unconventional elliptical shapes. The TELEVISA Services Building offers the same fascination as an expensive automobile parked downtown. It scintillates with well-crafted metallic joints, miraculously suspended planes of glass, and sheer roofing surfaces. Like an Alfa Romeo or a BMW, it performs as well as it looks thanks to the input of such foreign engineers as Ove Arup. Roofing panels made in Connecticut were assembled with local design ideas and combined with local craft. The tarnished black cement panels cladding the ground-level parking structure were rubbed by hand to achieve a unique mottled effect, a sort of smog camouflage at the base. The flaring oval section of the roof, which follows the tapering contours of the site, introduces a pudgy geometric figure to the district and shelters a spectacular vaulted dining space perched above the street. The bizarre shape of the TELEVISA building functions as a marketing icon for the company while deferring to the nearby warehouses, thus evoking the productive fabric of the city, but with a higher level of quality.

TEN's National School of Theater, Norten's most significant public commission, deftly explores an expressionist Mendelsohnian gesture—an immense rolling metal shed—with great technical assurance. Located at the intersection of two highways, the seven-story culvert provides a gigantic shield from the noise and fumes of the traffic and the hot western exposure. Open on its short sides to allow for natural ventilation, the shell encloses a series of independent volumes for the library, classrooms, and theater, and shelters truly "dramatic" semi-enclosed performance spaces. Without relying on historical forms of the theater, the disposition of monolithic volumes clad alternately in wood, stone, and glass and served by cascading terraces invokes the sort of spatial reflexivity that is the essence of theater. As with the TELEVISA building, the project involved international engineering consultants and elements available from a global economy. The steel ribs are held in place by pin joints, reminiscent of the engineering innovations of nineteenth-century bridges. Though produced in Mexico, the ribs were shipped to Houston to be bent into their elliptical shapes, while the slats of sequoia redwood, the most weather-resistant wood, were imported from California to shade the southern elevations. In its sophisticated structure, the National School of Theater touches the extremes of what is possible from international technology, yet its non-mechanically mediated, semi-enclosed environment offers the comfort of a traditional Mexican patio and serves to assimilate the building's alien form into the local area.

With the collapse of the Mexican economy in December 1994—perhaps the only thing not affected by the aforementioned endemic slowness—commissions on the scale of those two buildings cannot be expected for quite some time in Mexico City. TEN's most recent work has consequently been either for residences, international competitions, or university structures in the United States, where Norten has been a sought-after guest professor.

The inherent rationalism of Norten's layering design method is evident in his houses, including House X (1993), a palatial residence in a wealthy hillside Mexico City enclave, and House and Workshop H (1989), a small townhouse in a dense urban district of Valle de Bravo. House X was designed for the publisher of a weekly newsmagazine who is also an art collector. The site ramps up the hill. A series of long, deep eaves starts at the garden wall, continues to the balconies of the piano nobile, and is finally capped with a flared concrete-slab roof. The long wing of the L-shaped plan is equipped with conference rooms and a small theater; above this public level are the children's quarters. The short wing, which extends to the rear of the site, contains the master suite and is raised above an indoor-outdoor swimming pool. The circulation and services are sensibly placed at the intersection of the two wings, where there is also a double-height library. The program for the house is extravagant in terms of space and materials, yet the rational layout is quite economic in terms of construction and services. In its attention to shading and screening, the design conveys a discreet presence, much like the Los Angeles houses of Rudolf Schindler, in a neighborhood full of pompous, neocolonial monstrosities.

A more modest, but in almost all ways more satisfying, project is House LE (1994), designed by Norten for his own family. Built in a dense urban neighborhood, the house makes use of every centimeter of its tight lot while giving the impression of an open, generous space. This house is also L-shaped, with the servants' quarters and garage tucked into the short, street side, and the long axis continuously open to a split-level patio with a screened southern exposure. On the third level, where bedrooms are located and the house is most exposed, redwood slats—similar to those at the National School of Theater—hang from the eaves and shield the large expanses of sliding plate-glass. The free plan of the living level below flows around a translucent box for the kitchen. A surprise source of daylight and airflow comes from a half-meter slot adjoining the neighboring property on the north side. The successive lateral layers, from the street wall with its tactful slits to the wooden screens to the translucent interior partitions, create an atmosphere of glowing transparency.

Mexican architecture during the late twentieth century has in some ways been hostage to the reproduction of quaint forms, to sloppy craftsmanship, and to wild colors that please tourists but lead to new forms of colonial exploitation by discouraging the city's independent participation in modernity. During the past decade, Norten's technical competency and innovative reactions to the existing conditions of the city have authoritatively established that Mexican architecture can retain some of its gracefully slow regional identity in the use of such local typological devices as patios and wooden sunshades while also being precision-made and technologically innovative, hospitable to present-day speed and flexibility.

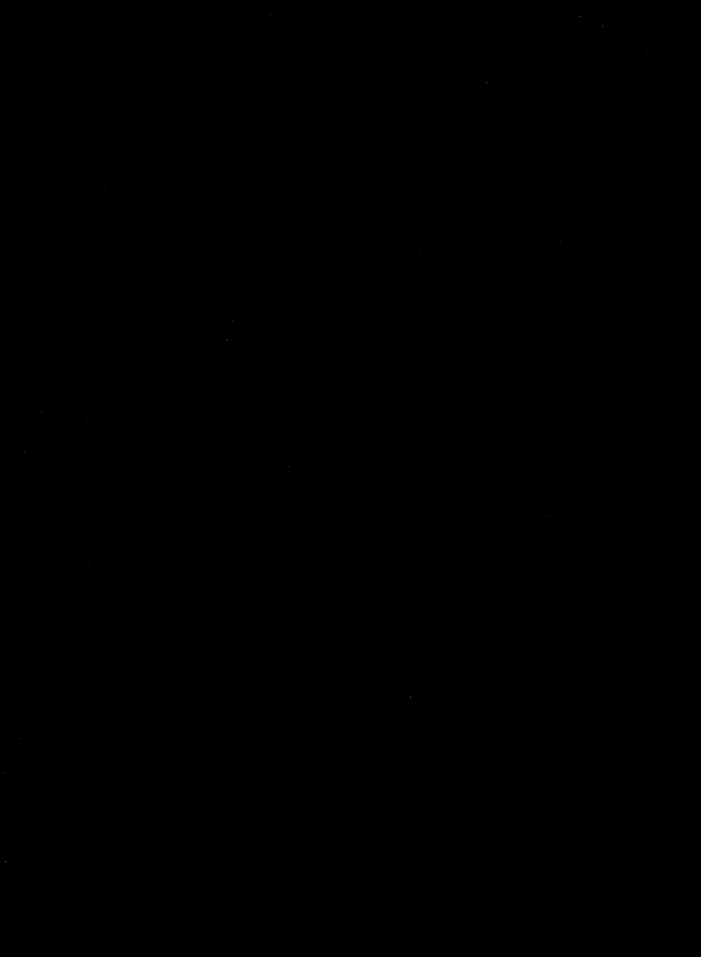

WORKS

LIGHTING CENTER

Colonia Roma, Mexico City
1988 (1989)

The triangular site of this 1940s flatiron building, on an important commercial street in Mexico City, is the result of the city's two overlapping grids, each a relic of a distinct historical moment and urban attitude. The idea behind the renovation of this former apartment building into a high-end lighting showroom was to express the modern confluence of disparate physical, temporal, and functional realities. We decided to preserve only what was basic, subtracting the extraneous, and we added elements that were necessary for updating the space's use and identity.

Once the building had been stripped to its elemental steel, concrete, and masonry structure, the new components and their various roles were distinguished materially as well as compositionally. The old, rough-textured masonry facade wears a new complexion of smooth, mullionless glass panels, mounted on a steel fretwork that tilts the translucent plane out, like a billboard. (Facing a busy thoroughfare, the reconfigured facade converts the whole building into an advertisement; a tiny building becomes a big billboard, in keeping with the urban scale.) On the interior, new surfaces of metal laminate, varnished wood, and polished marble were juxtaposed with the original concrete walls and floors in their unfinished state. The new respects the

old without compromising its independence, its own agenda. The dialogue between new and old, refined and raw, crafted and imperfect highlights the many layers of circumstance that are so characteristic of building in cities with complex physical legacies.

The introduction of new materials signals the contemporaneity of the interventions, while the nature of their insertion—all barely touch or cut through the existing structure—consciously alters the physiognomy of the building. The detachment of the new implies temporariness and the need for adaptability. Giving autonomy to these gestures was deliberate, meant to affirm the ephemeral nature of buildings and culture.

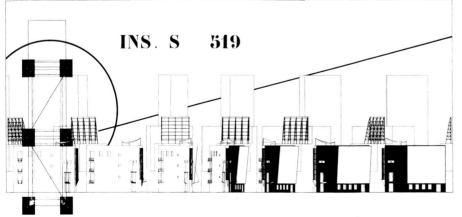

INS. S 519

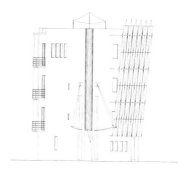

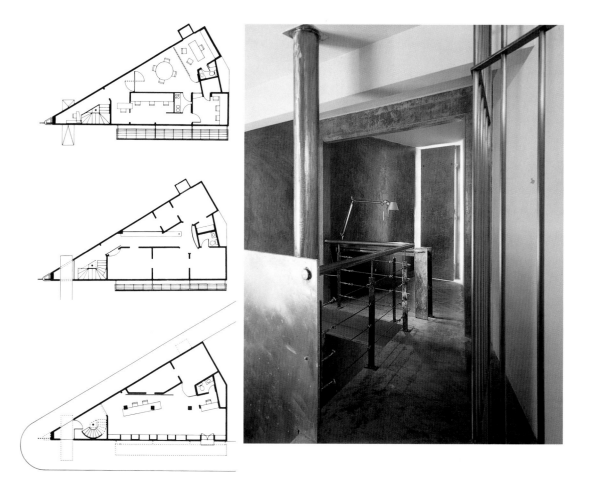

0 1 2   5   10 m

HOUSES N AND R

Cruz de Misión, Valle de Bravo
1989 (1990)

The looming natural features of this hillside site prescribed the plan and design of this pair of vacation houses, built for two childhood friends in a lakeside village 120 miles outside of Mexico City. Mountain and lake are such strong forces, at once attracting and opposing; one's back turns reflexively to what is massive and protective, while one's eye pulls naturally toward what is vast and open. Both houses rear up against the sheltering mass of the mountain and turn glazed sides to the clear waters of the lake below, while also maintaining a strong orientation toward each other. The two are essentially perpendicular to one another in order to create an enlarged communal space in between.

This shared outdoor space is a great amenity for the two households, but such an arrangement also requires a more clear delineation of—and hierarchy between—public and private and their relative importance. While each house responds uniquely in terms of orientation and proportions to the particular topographic conditions of its own site, the general plans of the two houses are similar, with the ground floor given over to guest quarters and the middle floor, which opens to a shared garden terrace, devoted to the living and dining rooms and kitchen. A double-height ceiling allows these more public rooms to flow vertically and continuously to the private sleeping quarters above, tucked away on the upper mezzanine.

Zoning regulations imposed a restricted palette of materials and finishes to preserve the town's "picturesque" appearance. The rules call for the use of local materials and traditional construction techniques as well as for the expression of "regional archetypes," and the result is a visually homogeneous community of whitewashed houses with brick walls, wood beams, and tile roofs. Forced respect for tradition via such style ordinances introduces its own brand of artificiality, and only heightens the fact that architecture today is as much about finding ways to circumvent restrictions as it is about developing appropriate solutions to unique and evolving needs. The challenge with this project was thus to create modern houses that address modern lifestyles within a constraining, tradition-bound code.

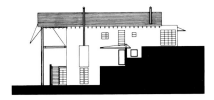

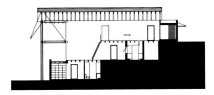

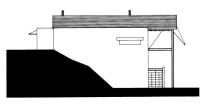

0 1   5   10 m

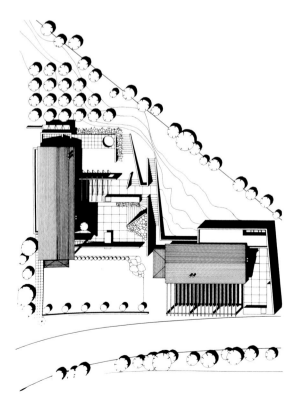

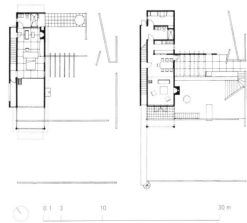

0 1 3   10   30 m

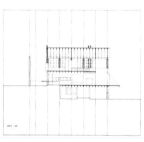

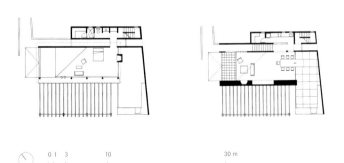

0 1 3   10   30 m

HOUSE O

Bosques de las Lomas, Mexico City
1990 (1991)

The design of this single-family house, located at the base of a hill in an affluent suburb of Mexico City, was a strong reaction to the lot's extreme proportions: a long and narrow slice of land, its twenty-one-meter length fronts a busy street, while its depth, a shallow eight meters, is delineated in the rear by a twelve-meter-high retaining wall.

Traditionally, buildings are conceptualized in terms of their plan, imagined from the ground up; in this case, with the vertical area exceeding the horizontal, we designed the house from the rear wall outward, essentially in section, like a scan or X ray. The result is a highly dynamic spatial sequence, defined by five staggered layers of vertical planes, some parallel to the street, others slightly skewed. These walls define the spaces and create circulation patterns; they delineate movement and the progression from public to private. Each plane retains a unique material, color, shape, and geometry to emphasize the divisions and intercourse between the various zones. The mixed material vocabulary and "slipped" placement of the planes express the incongruities, the dynamism, the instability of the house's urban context.

The phalanx of walls that guards the interior realms from the street stands in marked contrast to the transparent walls on the short ends of the house. Offering views toward the neighbors' gardens and exposure to the sun, these two sides are completely glazed, and both lead to outdoor patios that encourage the interior to spill out, elongating the house and its sight lines. With careful sections, openings, sequences, and circulation, this house extracts the most from a shallow space.

The impulse to remove private dwelling spaces from the intensity of the world outside informs many of our residential designs. Unlike the suburban model of object houses that are exposed on all sides, urban dwellings are more introspective, more concerned with carving out practical and personal domestic havens than with making symbolic statements.

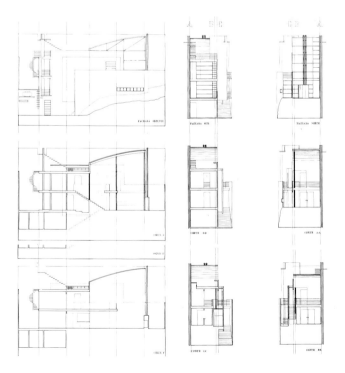

PLANTA ALTA

PLANTA BAJA

SOTANO

0 2 4   10   20 m

ALLIANCE FRANÇAISE

Lindavista, Mexico City
1990 (1992)

The Alliance Française, an institute dedicated to promoting French culture, in Mexico City occupies a classic urban lot; midheight buildings abut the sidewalk and each other. The spatial needs of the Alliance Française fell roughly into two categories: a theater, cafeteria, library, and gallery space were required for the building's more public component, while classrooms and administrative offices needed more seclusion. We built two separate volumes to address these differing needs, logically placing them at opposite ends of the site. In front, completing the street line, is a four-story volume with a gestural arcade; it houses the various public functions, which are accessible at multiple points via a fire-escape-like sequence of stairs. At the back of the lot is the block of classrooms and offices (with a small private rear patio that acts as a lightwell).

The two solid masses create a third volume, of equal size, between them, an unbuilt space that serves the dual purpose of dividing and unifying the structures that frame it. This transitional zone is filled with stairs and bridges fitted with enlarged landings and set in oblique directions; the result is a sort of multilevel plaza that forces unconventional paths and unpredictable encounters. The idea is to somehow express the compression of the city, and the way that objects in tension (characteristic of all densely packed urban spaces) yield a desirable vibrancy and energy. While the lot has a clear and straightforward structure overall, the spaces can be entered, used, and exited in variable and spontaneous ways. The project embodies the meeting of two orders—the strict orthogonal city grid and the random order created by its use, the flows of people through the building echoing the traffic and cultural interchange outside.

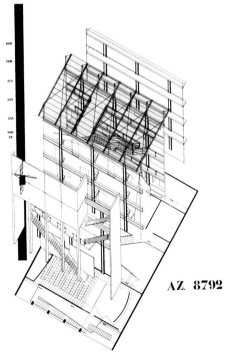

AZ. 8792

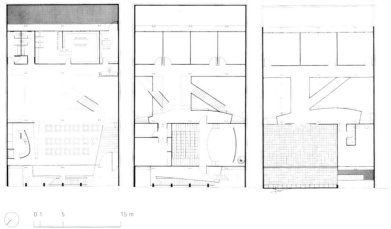

0 1   5   15 m

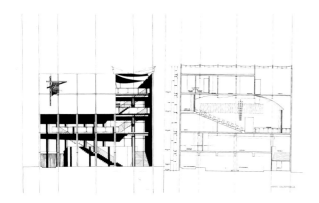

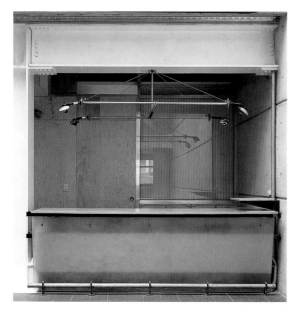

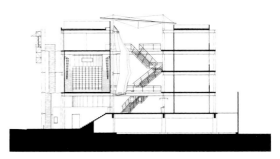

0 1   5   10 m

WORKERS HOUSING BRASIL 75

Mexico City
1991 (1992)

The Workers Housing project, developed by the Urban Infill Program for the Central Colonial District of Mexico City and funded by INFONAVIT (the National Funding Institute for Workers Housing), was an exercise in addressing the pervasive modern urban problem of inadequate and scarce affordable housing and in reclaiming and repairing the tears in the existing historic fabric.

On a deep narrow lot left over by the old grid of the city, we designed two four-story buildings facing each other in a modern interpretation of a traditional Spanish colonial *vecindad*, a form of low-rise multifamily courtyard housing. We gave the buildings a false front of stone, proportioned to the neighborhood standard in cursory fulfillment, if only ironically, of guidelines enforced in the historic center. Separated from the street by an iron gate, the neighborhood within a neighborhood is safely enclosed, with a shared public-private space that alleviates the compactness of the twenty-one units arranged around it.

Inherent in this housing model is the nurturing of community. The project's spaces are animated with various levels of social interaction. The twenty ground-level shop spaces are owned or operated by the buildings' inhabitants, further binding the residents to one another and to their context. By acknowledging certain cultural constants within a program that addresses contemporary lifestyles and standards of living, and with its modern layout and transparent spatiality, this project acts as a bridge between history and modernity, creating a comfortable place for its inhabitants within both local and universal contexts.

We built the housing on an extremely limited budget by using mostly off-the-shelf materials, such as standard masonry blocks, chain-link fencing, and stock lighting fixtures—inexpensive materials that should never be mistaken as "cheap." The value and elegance of the most basic of materials can emerge when they are assembled and detailed with care.

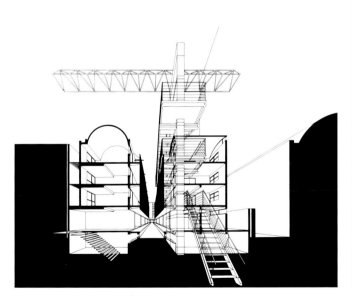

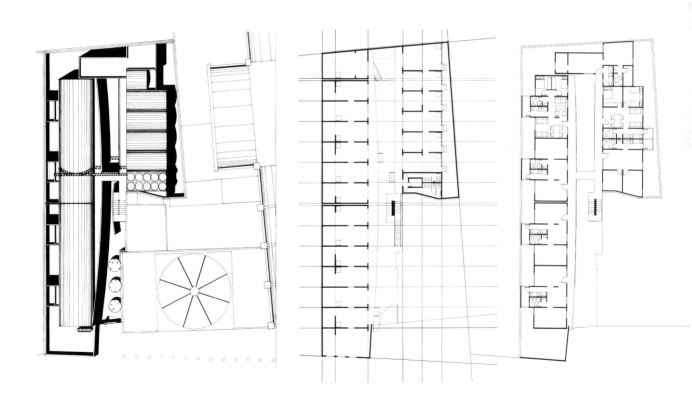

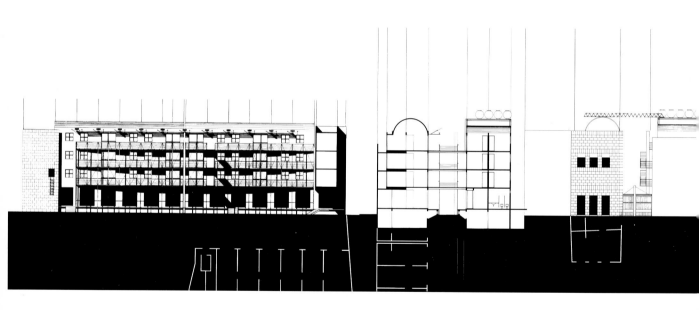

MODA IN-CASA

Lomas de Chapultepec, Mexico City
1991 (1993)

Moda In-Casa is a high-end furniture store located on the main stretch of an upscale neighborhood. Stringent zoning codes specify building heights and depths in order to keep the density and scale of the street low and pedestrian-friendly. Our critical response to such severe limits was to take them literally: we built the showroom to the maximum allowable height, width, and depth. With no desire to create an imposing, blocky object, however, we wrapped the building in the most nonexistent, ethereal enclosure possible. The facade and two side walls are entirely glazed; these double-tensed glass curtain walls hang with apparent detachment from an exposed steel-frame and concrete-slab structure. In making the membrane invisible, we ironically deny those imposed limits their

right to define the space; rather, the space is defined by the dynamics of the planes and lines within.

The building—in essence, a three-dimensional grid of walls and floors—owes its simplicity to its modular construction. A tight schedule demanded a design that would allow its various parts to be prefabricated in workshops throughout the city and assembled on site. The building was largely handcrafted (a "luxury" afforded by inexpensive local labor), which is surprising given its aesthetically and technically

refined, well-tooled appearance. The gridded structure lends well to movement and change, allowing the furniture to be framed and reframed. In effect, the building is a giant trophy case displaying the store's prized goods.

The building's transparency transfers great importance to light, which is capable of altering the showroom's atmosphere and the perception of its dimensions from moment to moment. The interior's fluctuating temperament stumps the building's strict structure; fluidity is favored over rigidity. The glass box is the generic embodiment of the modernist dream of trading the heavy and solid for the light and transparent, of abandoning stone for glass, and this ideal continues to preoccupy the profession. We strive to bring this fantasy ever closer to the edge, ultimately to fully detach the glass from the structure and give it complete independence, or to make it do more than seal and reveal, someday to carry more than its own weight.

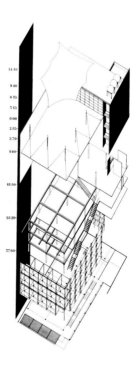

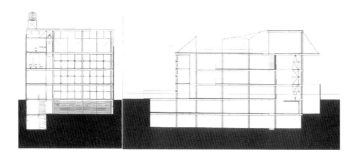

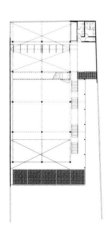 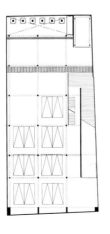  

0 5 10   20 m

FINSA OFFICES

Paseo de la Reforma, Mexico City
1993

Interior renovation jobs are always constrained by fixed factors. But these projects can be surprisingly liberating, for they are free of many of the pragmatic problems of construction. We see renovations as a chance to explore materials, details, and industrial design, and to reconcile old and new conditions.

A real-estate developer commissioned us to renovate a conventional office on the fourteenth floor of a 1960s modernist glass building, altering the existing space into their more stylish, image-conscious headquarters. We overlaid a completely nonorthogonal order onto the existing grid, first by skewing the primary axis, cranking the long corridor just a notch off from the other planes on the floor and from the building at large. Next we gave various walls a subtle tilt, in an overall strategy to muddle the sense of the actual limits of the space. To transform the space further and to emphasize its contemporary qualities, we chose materials that

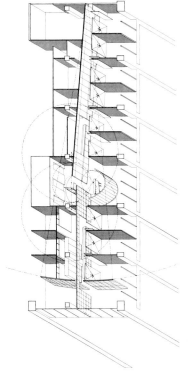

have a strong, distinctive presence, such as semiprecious blue Brazilian marble for the curved wall in the president's office and conference room, glass and stainless-steel laminate for the interior partitions, natural beech floors, and slate for the arching reception divider in the entrance foyer. Mixing orders and vocabularies forces a new understanding of an old space.

INSURGENTES THEATER

San José Insurgentes, Mexico City
1993 (1995)

The highly visible Insurgentes Theater, located on one of Mexico
City's most prominent boulevards,
is best known for the mosaic mural
by Diego Rivera that spreads across
its curving facade. In addition to
restoring the mural, this project
involved bringing the landmarked
1954 building to current structural codes, modernizing its me-
chanical, acoustic, and lighting
technologies, and creating new spaces for rehearsal, dressing,
makeup, wardrobe, and storage.

We felt that a simple formal and material vocabulary would
most appropriately express the new, improved workings of the
theater. Interior surfaces are flat and plain to reduce not only
acoustic but visual distractions, diverting complete attention
to the stage. In the auditorium, two sound reflectors flank the
smooth, wood-paneled side walls; they can be adjusted according
to the type of performance.

To create a more eventful entry foyer, we removed the old
central staircase—an overbearing feature that used too much
of the shallow space—and replaced it with a mezzanine-level
bar that allows the space and its activities to flow more openly
from floor to ceiling and from end to end. Moving the staircase to the side of the space also liberated prime center-mez-
zanine seating inside the auditorium.

We attached a completely new volume, housing the dressing, rehearsal, and storage rooms, to the north side of the old
building, alongside an entry ramp, which links the two buildings. The sloping ramp and the new service building are both
sheathed in austere aluminum-framed frosted-glass panels. The
addition and interior renovations are a straightforward architectonic expression of the functional improvements of the theater.

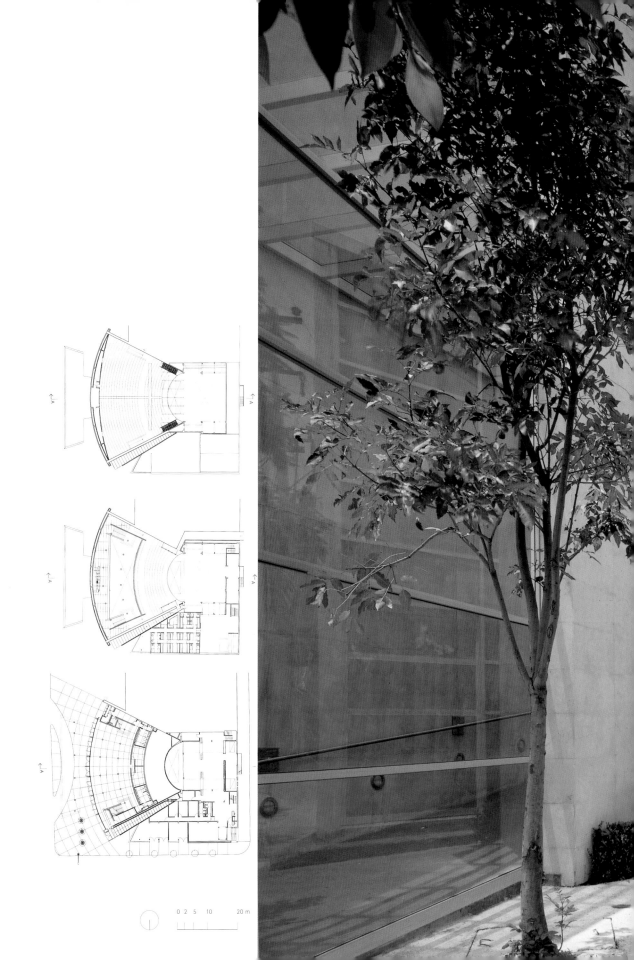

0 2 5   10   20 m

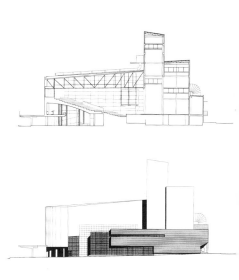

National School of Theater

Churubusco, Mexico City
1993 (1994)

The serenely sweeping metallic hull of the National School of Theater deflects the delirium of the two freeways that meet in a cloverleaf loop directly outside its door. Millions of motorists pass this point daily; seen primarily from a fleeting, high-speed perspective, the building demanded an immediately readable profile to give meaning to this particular place in the city.

Its striking curve, gleaming surface, and hangarlike scale compound the building's status as an urban icon and marker for the rest of the campus. (This building occupies the tip and most exposed site of the long campus, which includes five other newly built schools.) The arching steel-sheathed shell makes vague reference to the industrial warehouse sheds common to such urban peripheries, but, more significantly, it responds to the variety of functions it shelters.

The shell encloses an assemblage of volumes within, each a tectonic expression of a different category of use. The school's diverse program mirrors its inclusive approach to theater, which requires highly specific spaces for performance, lectures, and offices, as well as a gym and a library, and more flexible multipurpose rooms for rehearsals, studios, and workshops. In material and dimension, these spaces are endowed with unique textures, tones, personalities. For example, the ship-shaped library, which sails over the sheltered plaza below, sports an outer hull veneered in a tropical hardwood. Similarly, the sun-beaten southern facade is a three-story box screened by warm-toned redwood slats; containing rehearsal space and classrooms, this is the architectural antithesis of the glinty carapace on the flip side of the building.

These strongly articulated volumes are stacked in a seemingly ad hoc manner, although in fact they are logically arranged in terms of circulation and the relationships between various functions. The cavernous, continuous shell acts as a unifying backdrop for this amalgam of contradictory fragments, a proscenium for a diverse cast, each character charged with a different purpose but forced to share a stage. This main space is completely open on both ends like a tunnel. It is neither inside nor out; it is protected yet exposed; it is susceptible to wind but not rain. This space is a meeting ground not only for the building's users, but also for paradoxes and opposing forces, a balance of chaos and order.

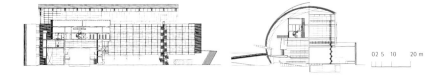

02 5 10   20 m

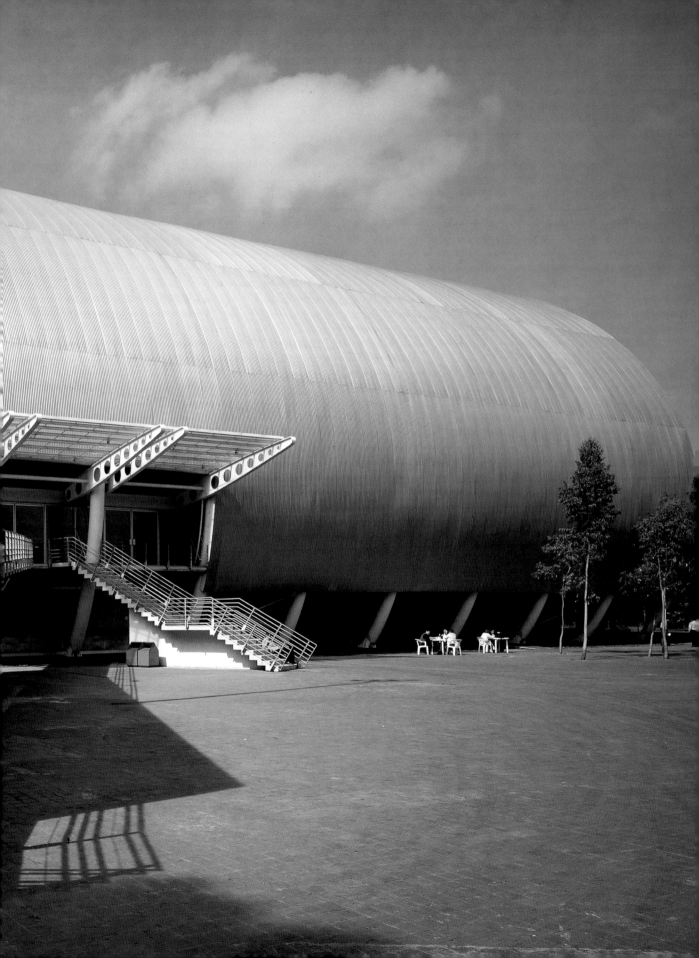

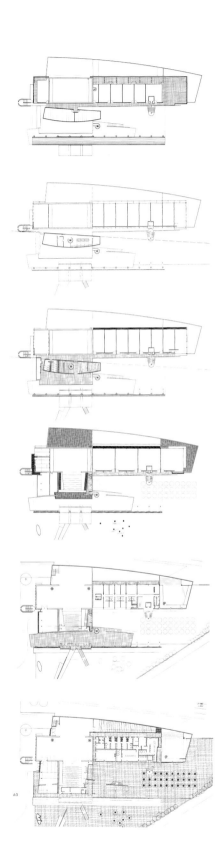

TELEVISA DINING HALL

San Ángel, Mexico City
1992 (1993)

The main production facility of TELEVISA, the largest television network in Mexico, is like a miniature city, with its own life, infrastructure, economies, patterns of use, and schedules. Lacking a dining hall to feed its thousands of workers—not to mention the space to build one—TELEVISA took our advice to use a two-story parking garage wedged in the corner of its property as the foundation for its

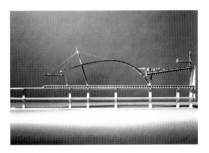

new cafeteria and multipurpose events hall. The limitations of the existing structure—its marginal siting, triangular footprint, and load-bearing capacity—informed the geometry and technology of the addition that was planted squarely on top of it.

Lightness, in terms of both weight and spirit, was the primary requirement for the addition. Built to its structural limits, the result is lively and self-possessed—a deliberate counterpoint to the static preconditions. A thin billowing shell of a roof is suspended from needle-nosed steel "stakes" pitched on existing weight-bearing nodes. These columns are angled to pull the metal-laminate roof outward; the supple curve of the roofline freezes the tense tilt. The roof cantilevers over a purposely ambiguous indoor-outdoor zone. The glazed southern facade enlarges the hall by bringing the expansive terrace and mountain views within its prospect.

To bring this edge of the studio closer to the rest of the property and to other buildings, we superimposed an artificial topography (featuring an aerial gangway, spiraling staircases, and ramping escalators) on the existing grades and paths of approach. An allée with benches and lightposts leads to the new exterior plaza at the foot of the cafeteria's northern "facade"—a flat white wall that serves the dual purpose of concealing the unsightly old structure and paying tribute to the client. It acts as a projection screen, with images swimming across its surface in constantly morphing self-reference. This plane is further enlivened by the two angular, boxed-in escalators that puncture its surface, carting employees over the frenetic visual threshold before delivering them into the vast great hall. The roof floats high overhead, undermining any sense of gridded order and conveying the edgelessness of mass media.

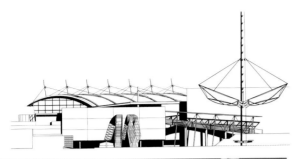

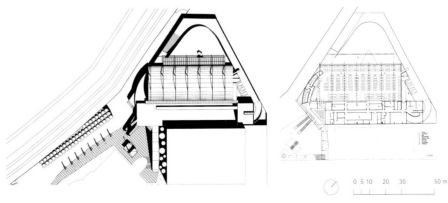

0 5 10   20   30   50 m

TELEVISA SERVICES BUILDING

Chapultepec, Mexico City
1993 (1995)

The contemporary city is suffused with ambiguous, undistinguished areas—nether zones at the overlapping peripheries of the multiple centers that have long since transplanted the single heart of the traditional city. Unnamed, multizoned, and without clear beginning or end, these areas present a challenging, conflicted context for any new design. Occupying several buildings throughout one such district, the television station TELEVISA decided to build a single facility to centralize a variety of uses and to promote a strong urban image befitting the company's new leadership.

The task of accommodating an eclectic program (ranging from a parking garage to offices, production facilities, and a cafeteria) while creating a unifying symbol is charged with inherent contradictions. Our building is actually two stacked forms: each cuts an independent figure to correspond to divergent categories of use, but both conform to the lot's unusual trapezoidal contours. (The odd-shaped lot, a result of haphazard street geometries, is bounded on one side by an eight-story network office building and a towering television antenna.) A boxy, monolithic base with hand-polished black concrete walls contains the ground-level parking garage and conventional offices above. This heavy volume is punctured only at two points, to allow pedestrian and vehicular entrance and exit. Perched atop this dark plinth is a shiny elliptical cylinder, a sloping, silvery blimp whose vaulting interior is devoted to the multipurpose dining hall. Also contained in this space, on an upper mezzanine partitioned off by frosted-glass walls, are private executive dining, conference, and club rooms. The southern end of this cornerless vault is a glass section that is partially obstructed by an exterior zinc-walled and glass-canopied entrance ramp and foyer. The placement of this object is deliberate, intended to diffuse the harsh light, spreading it along the lip of the continuous curve.

The rectilinear base preserves the scale of the low buildings and narrow streets of the immediate neighborhood. Meanwhile, the soaring aluminum-paneled shell alludes to an industrial vernacular and also represents a technically expedient method of construction. The meeting point of these two contrasting forms is a glassed-in floor of offices for employee services (bank, benefits, and so forth), its perimeter traced by an open, canopied terrace. This formless transition, by which the curve of the shell turns in on itself and disappears, gives the impression that the upper volume is floating.

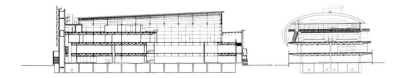

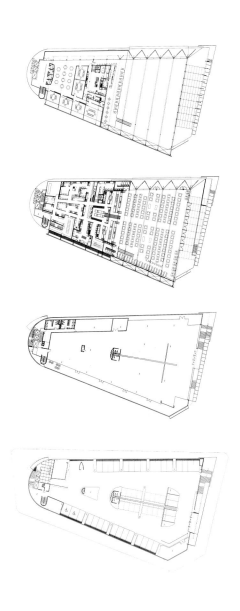

0 2 5   15   20 m

HOUSE X

Lomas de Chapultepec, Mexico City
1993 (1995)

On a sloping site in an exclusive, wooded residential area of Mexico City, we were commissioned to build a twenty-seven-thousand-square-foot house for a businessman and art collector and his family. Though the house has a large street presence, it remains dis-

creet and introspective, blind to the outside world. Oriented inward, the three-story L-shaped house is designed around a private outdoor garden court, in a modern rendition of the traditional courtyard plan.

The design exploits the lot's topography, which ascends nearly five meters from front to back. The long end of the L shape climbs through the site, its spaces defined by perpendicular planes and level changes (each floor steps a half-level into the site). This section contains the public rooms, beginning with the tall entrance foyer, which leads downstairs into the belowground theater, library, and service rooms, or upstairs a half-level into the formal living room, dining room, and kitchen. Toward the rear patio, this middle level is entirely open and accessible, in contrast to the completely closed stone walls facing the streets. The top, third floor contains the children's bedrooms, a study, and a broad corridor that overlooks the garden below. The widened circulation zones double as galleries to exhibit the homeowners' extensive sculpture collection.

The short end of the L plan defines the rear boundary of the lot. The two wings intersect at an indoor-outdoor swimming pool, which fills the corner of the lot, the concrete boundary walls descending directly into the water. The pool disappears beneath the short wing, where it is joined by a room that is used for entertaining. This level opens to the terrace. The pool, living room, and outdoor garden thus comprise a continuous space, which is covered by a glass roof and visible from the gallery corridor adjacent to the master bedroom on the level above.

The long block of the L serves as an experience buffer, its many layers filtering the procession from the hard spaces of the street to the soft spaces of the home and garden. The expression of these spaces is crucial—articulated not in terms of volumes, but of planes. The house's rational layout and construction lend well to the layering of planes, both opaque and transparent, varying the sight lines and movement through the house.

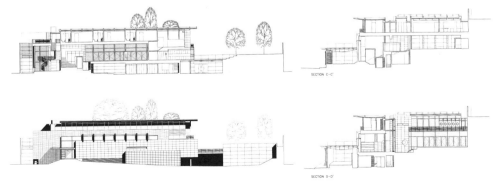

SECTION C-C'

SECTION D-D'

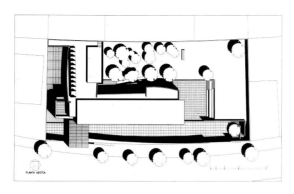

PLANTA AZOTEA

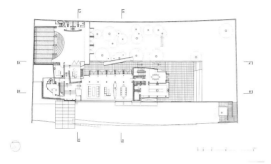

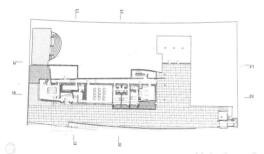

BASEMENT LEVEL

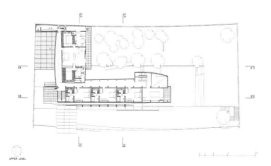

UPPER LEVEL

0 2 5   10   20 m

HOUSE LE

Condesa, Mexico City
1994 (1995)

For this prototypical urban residential lot
in an older and denser section of Mexico
City, we took an atypical approach while
still reinforcing some traditional dwelling
patterns and maintaining the street's tex-
ture. These shoebox-shaped lots, tightly
bound by party walls, are most frequently
front-loaded, with built volumes aligned
to the street and opening to gardens or
terraces at the rear. But this configuration
produces a back-to-back "promiscuity";
residents are always at risk of exposure. With
a desire for privacy as well as for a relationship with the outdoors, we too built
on one half of the lot, leaving the other
void, but we divided the lot longitudinally

rather than transversally. The result is a long and narrow building,
essentially one room wide, with spaces lined up in a straight shot,
front to back. The house is as rational in arrangement as in construction, a reflection of the compactness of the lot, the limited
budget, and the simple needs of the family that lives here.

The house is layered in slender sections that run the entire
length of the house, perpendicular to the street; the sequence of
longitudinal zones is subtly transcribed onto the otherwise chaste
facade. Parallel to the north party wall is a thin stratum of storage (which also acts as a sound and climate buffer) encased in a
smooth plane of wood, followed by a long, uninterrupted corridor
from which the living rooms radiate. This is the widest zone of
the house, containing a library/family room and service areas on
the ground floor, kitchen and living areas on the middle floor, and
private bedrooms on the third. This zone is bounded by a wall of
glass, a transparent transition to the outdoors that is softened by
the shade of the overhung roof. The upper, more exposed half of
the house has another layer, a handmade screen of redwood louvers that shields the most private rooms without cutting them

off from exterior views. Patios on the ground and second floor constitute the next layer, open spaces that terminate with a tall, ivy-covered party wall at the boundary line.

Closed to the street and completely open and transparent inside, the house fulfills its inhabitants' simultaneous desires to live in the city and enjoy its intensity and energy while also maintaining privacy and intimacy. Though compact (three hundred square meters), the house feels large due to its clear circulation and continuous spaces, which are divided by simple, domino-like planes. The straightforward construction and configuration also lends well to adaptation—an increasingly important provision for modern houses.

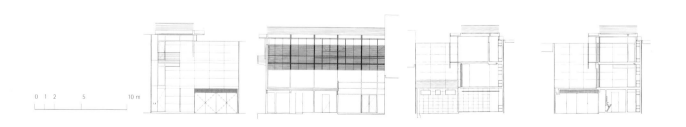

0 1 2   5   10 m

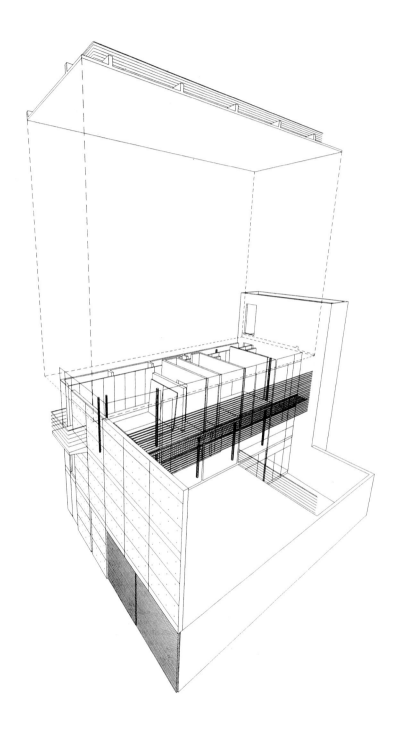

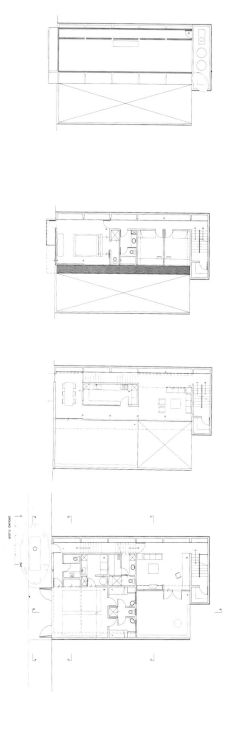

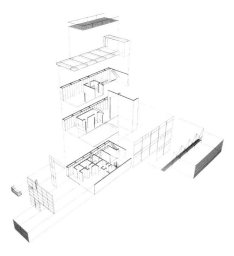

GROUND FLOOR

0 1 2   5   10 m

JAGUAR DEALERSHIP

Santa Fe, Mexico City
1997
Gilberto Borja, associate architect

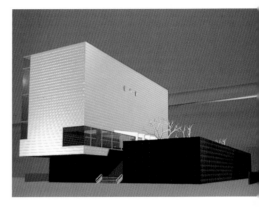

Visibility from the distant road was the main charge of the Jaguar Dealership, located on the sparsely developed edge of Mexico City where upscale office parks and shopping malls are just beginning to cluster around newly paved expressways. We gave the building a clearly legible form, stacking two strongly geometric boxes one upon the other: a gleaming, four-story-tall vertical balances precariously on a dark, low-lying horizontal. The upper volume is clad in corrugated metal, its eye-catching surface only minimally interrupted: three portholes perforate one facade while two glazed swaths are cut out, one wrapping a corner top to bottom to convey the full height of the atrium showroom, and the other tracing the ground level to display the Jaguars on the floor. This semitransparent viewing case is cantilevered over the solid submass; it juts toward the street, dangling its tempting goods before the commuting consumer.

The lower, limestone-clad volume contains the garage. It is backed into the base of the hill and partially sunken into the site, providing a firmly anchored foundation for the towering block above. The entrance to the showroom is situated directly beneath the suspended block, as is the head of the ramp that descends into the garage. Visitors cross this "portico" to enter a dramatic, three-story-high, skylit showroom. The windowed offices at the rear of the space mimic the stepped exterior section, with a glassed-in conference room that hangs from the ceiling like a lookout platform and steps back in two levels to rejoin the showroom floor.

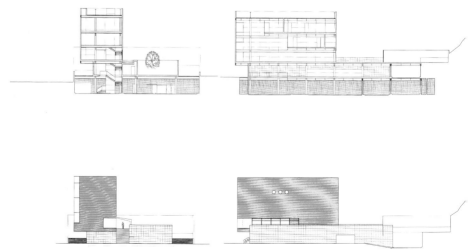

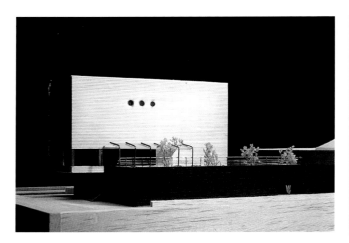

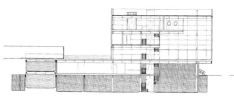

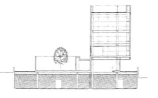

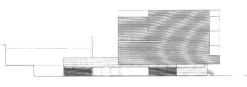

0 2 5   10 m

165

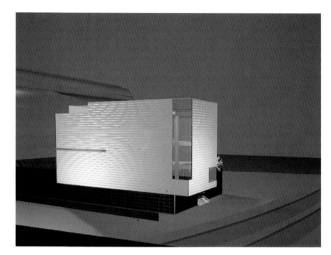

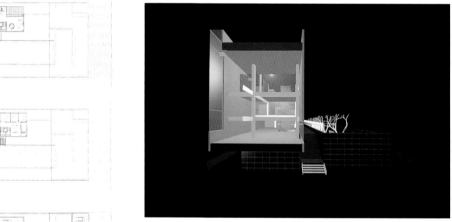

Projects and Works in Progress

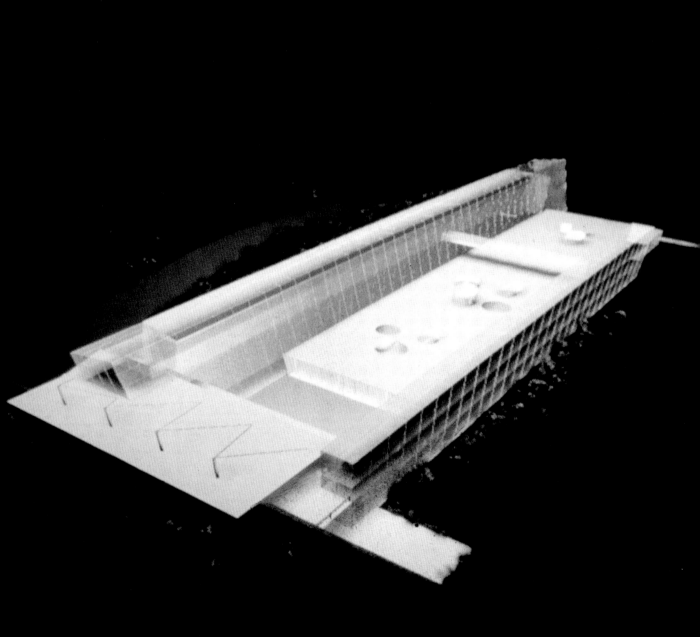

MUSEUM OF SCIENCES

Chapultepec Park, Mexico City
1995 (in progress)

On a densely wooded section of Chapultepec Park in Mexico City, this new, forty-nine-thousand-square-meter museum is to replace an existing museum and house its permanent collection as well as expand its program with a store, restaurants, open plaza, and educational and research facilities. An isolated object in the thick of trees, this scheme

experiments with translucent and transparent lines and planes to provide for spatial and programmatic flexibility.

The new museum is a low-lying structure comprised of three chief volumes: the outermost, canopied, rectangular slab contains all the public areas, including the entrance lobby, store, and temporary exhibits. Behind its glazed length is a vast, submerged colonnaded hall, which houses the permanent collection as well as storage space and an auditorium. The expansive roof of this opaque plinth serves as an outdoor exhibition space and terrace. The rear volume, also transparent, contains the library, classrooms, and laboratory; its canted facade encloses a bright corridor that runs parallel to the permanent exhibition space. The varying degrees of transparency and translucency of this assemblage of prisms and solids address the different activities within them, while also extending the fluctuating conditions of clarity and shadow, visibility and opacity, in the surrounding forest.

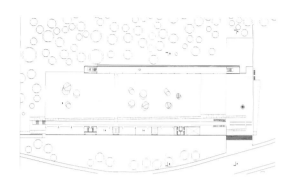

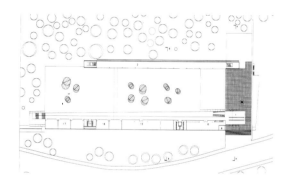

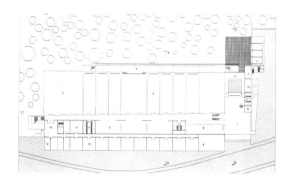

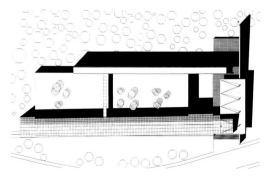

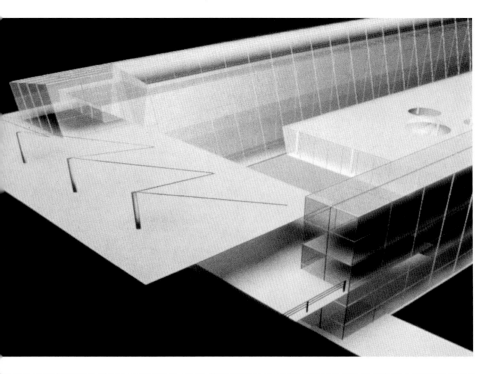

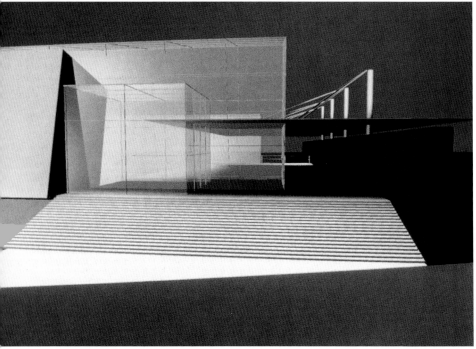

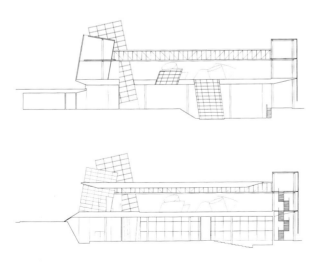

House RR

Desierto de los Leones, Mexico City
1996 (in progress)

The program and budget for this house—on a seventeen-by-twenty-one-meter lot in a neighborhood of Mexico City—demanded a clear, straightforward order to maximize the lot's tight dimensions. The L-shaped plan is a practical residential model for dense urban conditions because it allows the mass of the house to act as a shield from the frenetic street while creating a private,

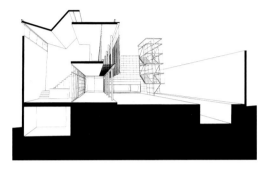

protected interior zone that maintains a correspondence to the outdoors. In this single-family house, the short end of the L continues the street's line of townhouses, while the slightly longer end extends perpendicularly from the street, dividing the lot lengthwise as a response to its orientation and pronounced level variation. (This section of the house shares a party wall with its neighbor to the north and, with a glass curtain wall, is open to the courtyard to the south.)

Filling in the irregularly sloped bottom level are the garage and entrance on the short section, and the service and laundry areas along the long section. The entrance leads to a staircase encased in a tall, glass-paned tower. On the middle level, the living room, dining area, and kitchen spill outward to the rear courtyard. The long wing terminates with a double-height study, which is shared by the master bedroom above. The top level also contains the family room (at the top of the glazed stair tower), which is linked to the bedrooms by a transparent bridge. This more intimate and exposed upper level is protected from outside views and the strong southern sun by a plane of cedar louvers. The spaces of the house are defined by the layering of planes along both axes, each made of a unique material and tectonically expressing its function and location in the house. These carefully sequenced planes also act as a filter for the external world, culminating in the more introspective core of the house and garden.

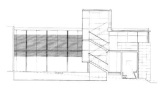

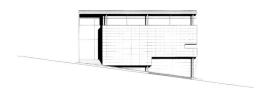

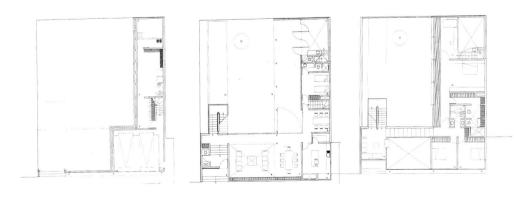

0 1 2   5   10 m

179

Nursing and Biomedical Sciences Building

Houston, Texas
1996 (unbuilt)

Our submission to this limited competition was an important exercise because it offered us the chance to explore various ideas that have long been of interest. Intended to be a state-of-the-art teaching center for the University of Texas Health Science Center at Houston, the Nursing and Biomedical Sciences Building (NBSB) called for the integration of an inspiring learning environment with sophisticated computer networking and information technology. New technologies are steadily rendering work "placeless"; information can be transferred and departments linked invisibly. Posing a con-

tradiction of sorts, the NBSB was simultaneously programmed to be strongly grounded and local—to be a centralizing facility that would complete a pedestrian sequence between the neighboring Social Health Building, an adjacent beautiful parkway, and nearby parking lots. Our design scheme embodies the intersection of technology and architecture, of local and universal processes and place.

We divided the building into three discernible segments: two rectangular slab buildings—one opaque, the other transparent—are arranged parallel to and staggered from each other. The slipped placement of the two buildings creates plazas at both ends, unbordered spaces that bring the park closer to the buildings. The academic building is envisioned as a transparent volume, imbued with light and openness as places of learning should be. The opaque volume contains the administrative wing and accommodates more private activities. The pressure between the two volumes creates an exploding geometric crystal atrium out of the intervening space. This faceted, luminous breezeway is an accessible crossroads, drawing people from the campus at large. A departure from most campus buildings, which deter non-university traffic and obstruct the landscape, our building, with its crystalline midsection, serves as a thoroughfare and meeting ground for students, faculty, administrative staff, and the general public alike. The ground level of the atrium is further animated by a café, bookstore, copy center, retail venues, and daycare center. This clear section also exposes the nature of the building's structure and workings, which includes passive cross-ventilation and other energy-saving systems.

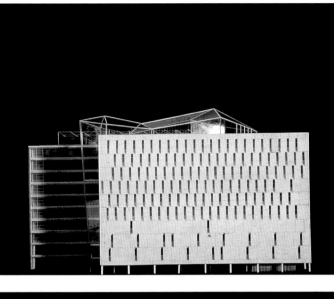

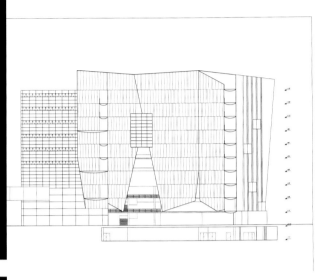

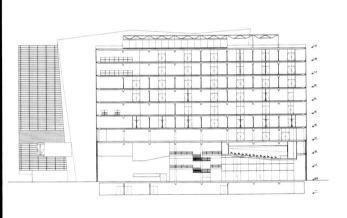

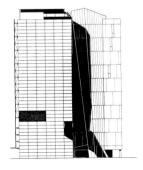

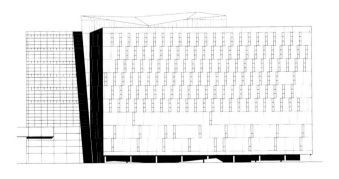

0 2 3 7 15 m

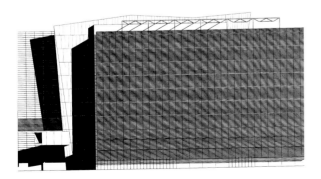

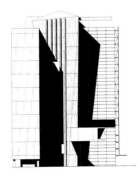

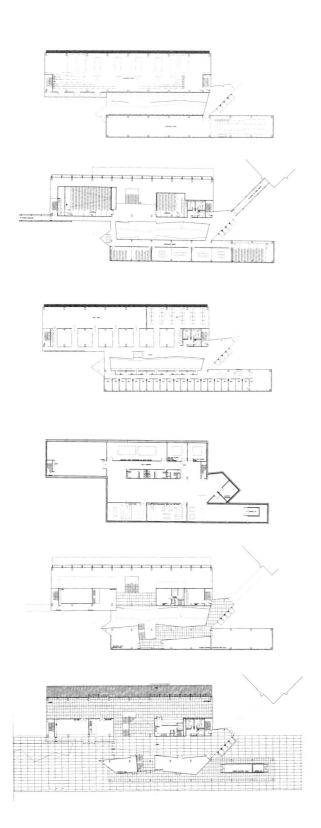

HOTEL LAMARTINE

Polanco, Mexico City
1996 (in progress)

On a fashionable commercial street lined with high-end stores and office buildings, we were commissioned to convert a five-story apartment building into a forty-room boutique hotel. The new services and amenities—such as a swimming pool, sauna, bar, and restaurant—will be added to the roof, but otherwise only minor changes will be made to the 1950s building, which is structurally and functionally sound. The old structure nonetheless gains an entirely new identity with a new wrapper, a frosted-glass box of mullionless rectangular glass panels floating several feet from the original facade. Sandwiched between the new and old facades are the original balconies and new breezy metal-mesh corridors, which will be linked by stairways.

From a distance, the clean new facade appears to be an expressionless mask, but this impression is undone at closer range as the shadows of walkways and the outline of the tension rods holding the panels in place become visible. Small, randomly distributed unfrosted squares and rectangles are the new facade's only adornment. These strategically stingy transparent slots give each room controlled views to the city beyond, framing the desirable and screening out the unsightly. At night, the entire building will appear as a lantern with a changing checkerboard pattern of illumination, varying with the occupancy of the rooms.

The rooms themselves, looking outward to two planes of floor-to-ceiling glass (the inner transparent, the outer translucent), are imbued with natural light all day while maintaining complete privacy. The decor of the rooms mirrors the austerity of the outer enclosure: only a bed occupies the space, with everything else (television, closets and drawers, and a Murphy desk) concealed behind a polished paneled wall. This minimalist aesthetic enlarges the experience of the otherwise compact rooms.

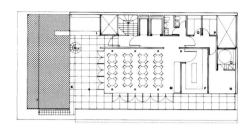

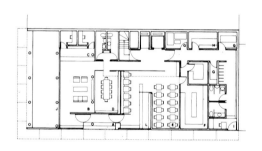

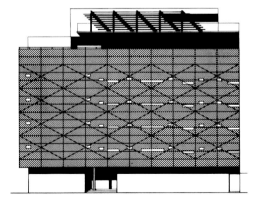

0 1 2 3 5   10 m

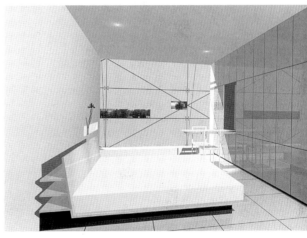

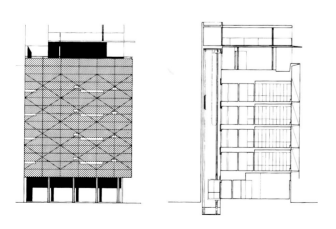

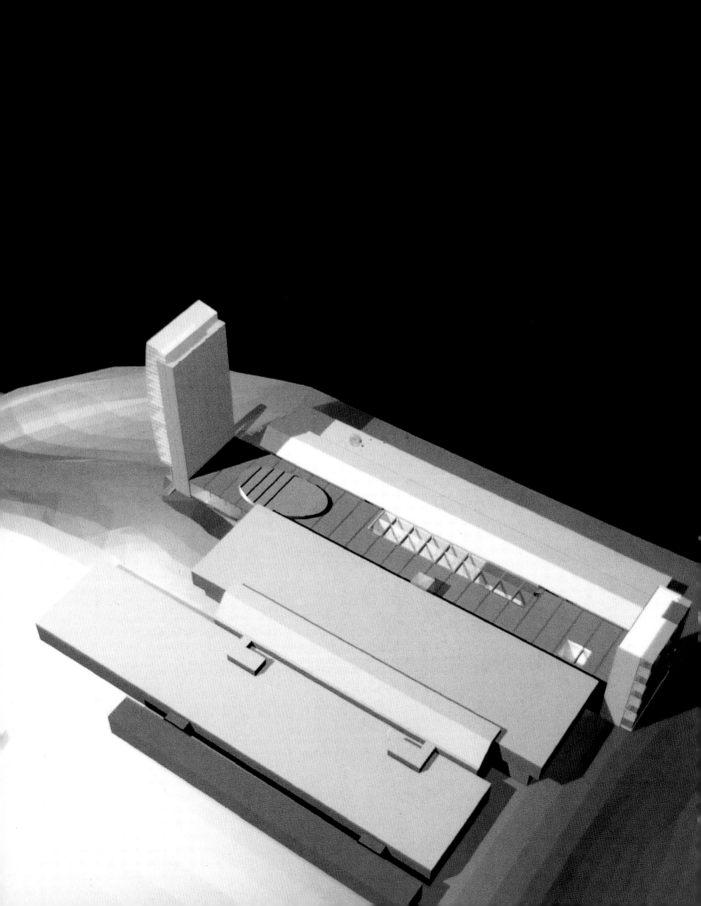

College of Art and Architecture

Ann Arbor, Michigan
1997 (in progress)

The College of Art and Architecture at the University of Michigan is located on its North Campus, a far-flung suburban satellite of the campus proper. Distinctly un-campuslike, it is more accurately a collection of discrete structures separated by parking lots and built abruptly against pedestrianless sidewalks. The college currently occupies three long, low, and narrow buildings, which are arranged in parallel rows, aligned with the street. They are accessed and linked by two main corridors that cut through them perpendicularly. With various and unceremonious entry points, the buildings have neither common areas nor any legible spatial order or hierarchy.

We were commissioned not only to enlarge the College of Art and Architecture (adding an auditorium, gallery space, offices, and studios) but also to reprogram the entire complex. We decided to fill in the vacant space between two of the existing volumes with a platform, a neatly added volume that will serve as the new center of the complex. This space, a former outdoor patio, had been mostly ignored because of the way the original corridors cut through it. In roofing it and also planting two new structures on its extreme ends—one tall administration building and a shorter residence unit—we have given the new quadrangle clear boundaries. We will also bring all the public activity spaces, such as the cafeteria, auditorium, exhibition space, and copy center, to its edge, further promoting its use as a gathering space.

In devising a new system of circulation, the most important thing was to funnel everyone into the building complex via a single point of entry. The new main entrance is on axis with the long quadrangle, located at the base of the new administrative tower,

which is lifted on stilts and thus acts as a sort of portico. Beyond this entrance foyer is the auditorium, a freestanding oval volume set obliquely in the middle of the space. Visitors pour around both sides of its wood-veneered walls into the open quadrangle, and may take the old corridors to the studios and classrooms.

In redistributing the interior, we reserved the large rooms in the existing buildings for workshops, laboratories, studios, and class-rooms, and concentrated all of the offices in the administrative tower. To overcome people's reluctance to move their offices into mid- or high-rise towers (many dislike the anonymous experience of pushing an elevator button and being deposited into indistinct hallways on identical floors), we created smaller, more manage-able "buildings" within the building: we clustered two or three floors (according to department) around a common lounge area that is accessible only to its cluster. With secondary paths inde-pendent to each department, this strategy nurtures a sense of community within each cluster and represents an alternative ap-proach to the typical relentlessly stacked corporate-tower type.

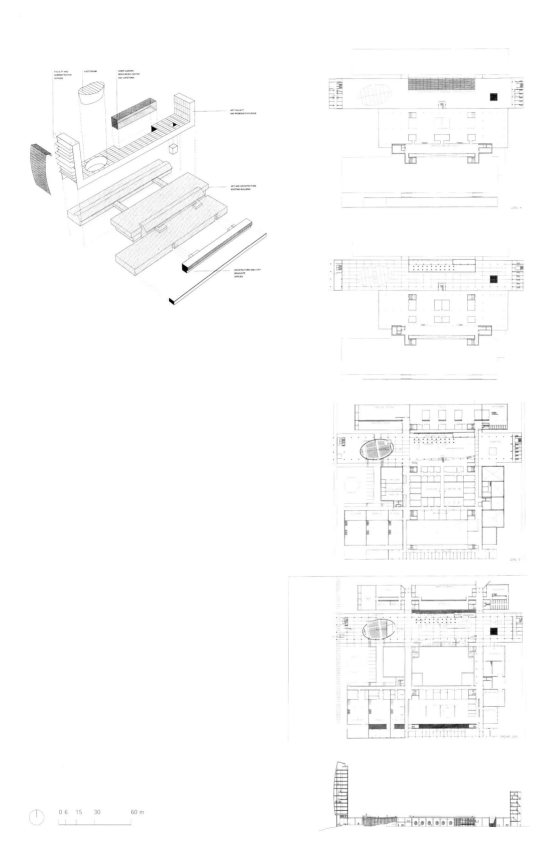

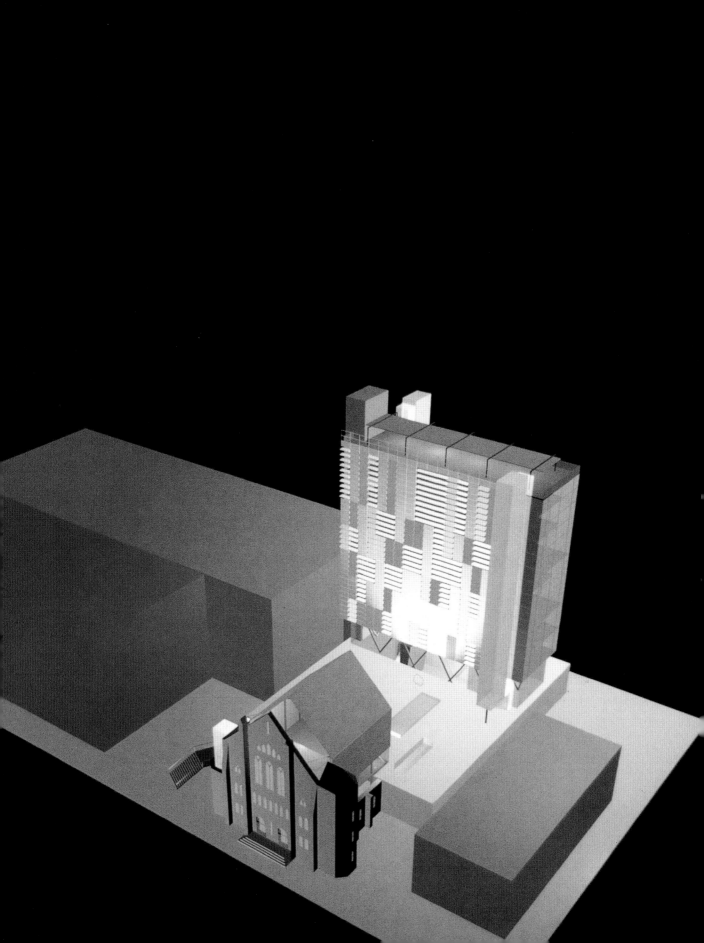

ADDAMS HALL AND FINE ARTS BUILDINGS

Philadelphia, Pennsylvania
1997 (in progress)

Across the street from the main campus of the University of Pennsylvania is the site for the new Graduate School of Fine Arts and its exhibition gallery, Addams Hall. The lot, totaling twenty-five thousand square feet, spans the width of the block and is fronted by the remains of an early-twentieth-century neo-Gothic church that was severely damaged by a fire in 1996. We divided the program into three parts, the first involving the construction of Addams Hall on the site of the old church. Required to salvage the three surviving walls, we decided to make a clean insertion of the new structure—a simple glass cube with an A-line roof that echoes that of its precursor—inside the old stone walls rather than grafting a building to or around them. This strategy allows us not to contend tangibly with the remains of the church, as a conventional addition might have entailed.

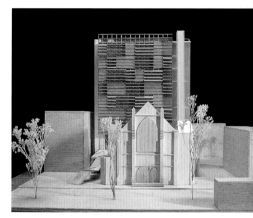

The church's original street-level entrance now leads into the primary exhibition space of the new Addams Hall. The addition leads in turn to the second phase of the project, a flat, spreading volume that completely fills the middle of the site. One story above grade, this rectangular base contains flexible studio spaces that are arranged on axis with the formal gallery in Addams Hall. Doorways and movable walls allow these studios to double as exhibition galleries, extending continuously from the Addams Gallery. The below-grade level of the expansive middle volume is given over to workshops and studios for the "heavy" arts, such as work in metal, wood, ceramic, and glass, while the roof serves as an outdoor plaza. The public may access the elevated terrace directly from the street via a set of stairs, while the school community may reach it from the second-floor cafeteria of Addams Hall.

The central volume provides the foundation for the third phase of the project: an eight-story slab devoted to faculty offices, lounges, and studios for the "lighter" arts, such as painting and drawing, which are fittingly raised in the air. To avoid the anonymous feeling of a corporate office tower, the floors are clustered to create three minibuildings stacked within the building. These clustered floors share double-height lounges located at the sunny, glazed end of the building. These subsections are each devoted to different departments and maintain their own independent circulation.

Though the buildings have not yet been detailed, the two pronounced objects on the site are both partially sheathed, glazed enclosures—one in the old heavy stone walls, the other in lightweight wood-slatted louvers that mitigate the brightness of the sun. By dividing the overall program into three parts, the church becomes a freestanding object and the tall slab a backdrop, both perched on an inconspicuous plateau in an arrangement that endows the school with added open space.

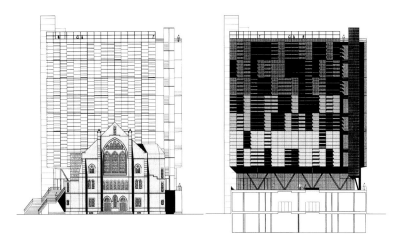

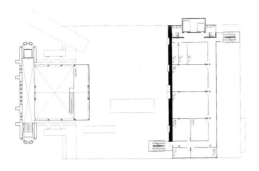

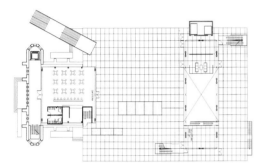

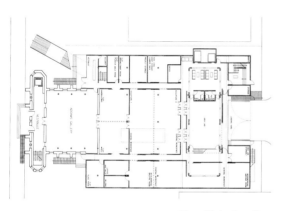

0 1 2 4 8 16 m

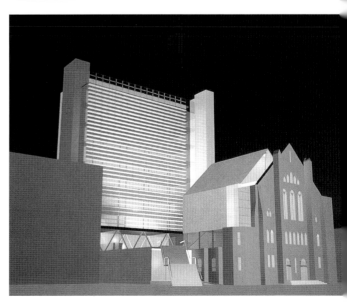

EL CAMINO REAL HERITAGE CENTER

Socorro, New Mexico
1997 (in progress)
Holmes-Sabatini and Associates,
associate architects

The purpose of the El Camino Real Heritage Center is to celebrate the history of the state of New Mexico through the stories of the people who have traveled this famous trail during the three hundred years of its existence. El Camino Real (the royal road) was the main thoroughfare connecting Santa Fe, the northernmost location of the Spanish empire in the Americas, to Mexico City, the empire's capital.

The center will be located on a breathtaking plateau overlooking a beautiful long valley through which El Camino Real once passed, a pristine desert site a few miles south of the city of Socorro. A very abstract horizontal parallelogram will be positioned at the edge of the plateau, barely touching the ground. One-third of this prism will be cantilevered over the cliff at the edge of this built mesa, overlooking the valley and El Camino Real in the distance. This object, clad in local limestone, will convey to the observer a sense of discomfort and fragile equilibrium, in contrast to the serenity of the desert.

The long sides of the prism are practically blind, with very small punctuated openings accentuating specific views from the inside and allowing controlled light from the east and west into the various spaces. The short sides are transparent, accentuating the longitudinal nature of the scheme and the long-axis circulation pattern of the building.

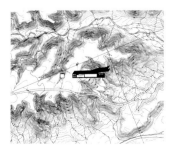

The building is entered from the north, into a ground-level foyer, from which the information desk and museum store can also be accessed. An indoor-outdoor ramp will bring visitors to the upper lobby, separated from the rest of the museum by an upper courtyard. The introductory exhibition space will be entered through the courtyard, as will the lobby of the small auditorium that will be used for projecting videos to introduce visitors to the state's history. The sloped floor of the auditorium will allow visitors to exit onto the ground floor, where the exhibitions will be located.

The south facade is totally transparent, leading into a walled-in open terrace overlooking the valley and the historic site of El Camino Real. The exhibition will be observed after contemplating El Camino Real and the astonishing views from the terrace, bringing visitors through the collection and back to the entry space through the store.

The library is located on the roof of the auditorium, overlooking the terrace and the main exhibition gallery. Administration offices are situated underneath the lobby, with two small apartments above, all connected by a private staircase.

A sunken space housing food facilities and a place for relaxation will be located north of the center's entrance-exit, on axis with the building. This recreational area will be encountered by visitors on the way back to their cars.

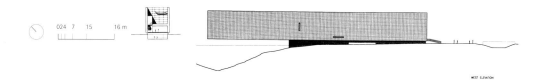

WEST ELEVATION

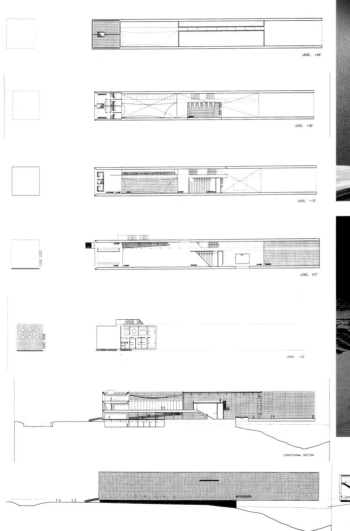

LEVEL +40'

LEVEL +30'

LEVEL +15'

LEVEL 0'0"

LEVEL -12'

LONGITUDINAL SECTION

EAST ELEVATION

FURNITURE

DOING A PIECE OF FURNITURE IS SERIOUS STUFF, VERY SERIOUS STUFF.

—Jean Prouvé

Furniture design and architecture have developed on similar grounds and in many ways share a common history. Each enriches the other. Although the pursuits have very different conditions and scale, some of the problems are the same. An idea must be expressed, crystallized into solid three-dimensional form, and built. Several elements have to be assembled, thus introducing the potential for diverse problems to arise. Both disciplines take into account proportion, joints, materials, structure, and modes of construction. Like architecture, furniture gives form to utilitarian objects. On the other hand, furniture can be infinitely repeated and inserted into different locations. For us, however, it usually has a precise use and belongs to a particular space.

Immediacy is another aspect that divides furniture and architecture. A first furniture prototype can exist in several weeks, leading to a revised final prototype in a couple of months. With architecture, several years can stretch from design to construction. With furniture, the rapid movement from sketch to product allows an idea to be tested in a relatively short time and can even help in the much slower development of an architectural product.

Every material possesses intrinsic qualities that must be taken into account and utilized, such as temperature, reflectiveness, hardness, elasticity, and durability. Any furniture object is usually an assembly of different pieces that work together and complement each other. More important than the individual components are the general composition, the relationship between the different pieces, and the way they are put together. Architecture follows a very similar process, and doing one enriches the other. Learning about the use of a particular material and the detailing that goes with it is only gained in the actual doing.

Furniture needs its own identity; this comes not only from its function but can also be dictated by the construction process. The clarity of the original idea has to be strong enough to read in the final product, a clarity recognized not only in the definition of the materials but in the simplicity of structure and the way the two are joined together.

Designing furniture has contributed to our understanding of certain architectonic interests, and has also helped us to develop tectonic and constructive details. Our furniture work functions in some way as a kind of laboratory, through which experimentation and invention can take place, through which ideas can be tried, materials handled, structures clarified, and construction methods studied. Furniture design and construction has thus served not only in the obvious creation of objects but has also helped our architectonic purposes.

BERNARDO GÓMEZ-PIMIENTA

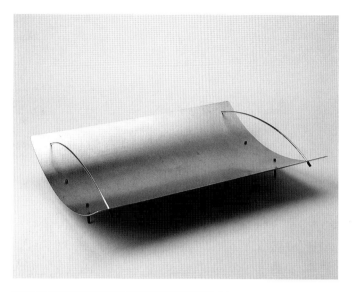

TEN Arquitectos

The firm was founded in Mexico City in 1985 by Enrique Norten. Bernardo Gómez-Pimienta joined the firm as a partner in 1987. Currently, TEN Arquitectos has fifteen members.

TEN Arquitectos has received several awards, including the Latin-American Prize, awarded by the International Association of Architectural Critics, in the Buenos Aires Bienal of 1993; *Progressive Architecture* awards, in 1994 and 1995; the Record Houses Award, in 1993; and various awards in the Mexican Bienales of 1990, 1992, 1994, and 1996.

TEN Arquitectos was invited to participate in the 1996 Venice Biennale and in the international exhibition "Presents and Futures", held in Barcelona in 1996 for the International Congress of Architects (UIA). The work of TEN Arquitectos has been shown in galleries and museums in Mexico, the United States, and Europe, both in collective and individual exhibits, and has been widely published throughout the world.

ENRIQUE NORTEN

Norten was born in Mexico City in 1954. He studied architecture at the Universidad Iberoamericana, in Mexico City, receiving his first professional degree in 1978. He earned his master of architecture degree from Cornell University, graduating in 1980.

Norten started his professional practice in Mexico City in 1981 as a partner of Albin y Norten Arquitectos S.C. In 1985, he founded the firm Taller de Enrique Norten Arquitectos S.C. (TEN Arquitectos).

Norten has been a professor of architecture at the Universidad Iberoamericana (1980–90), and a visiting professor at Columbia University in New York City (1991), Rice University in Houston (1993), and the Southern California Institute of Architecture in Los Angeles (1994). He was invited to teach at Cornell University as a Distinguished Visiting Professor (1994), and for the O'Neal Ford Chair in Architecture at the University of Texas at Austin (1996), the Elliot Noyes Visiting Design Critic at Harvard University (1996), and the Lorch Professor of Architecture Chair at the University of Michigan (1997).

Norten is a founding member of the magazine *Arquitectura*.

BERNARDO GÓMEZ-PIMIENTA

Gómez-Pimienta was born in Brussels, Belgium, in 1961. He obtained his bachelor of architecture degree from the Universidad Anáhuac, in Mexico City, in 1986. In 1987, he received his master of architecture degree from Columbia University, in New York City. Gómez-Pimienta joined TEN Arquitectos in 1987.

Gómez-Pimienta has taught architecture at the Universidad Iberoamericana (1987–88), at the Universidad Anáhuac (1989), and at the Universidad Nacional (1992–96), all in Mexico City. He was also a visiting professor at the Southern California Institute of Architecture (1994) and a visiting associate professor at the University of Illinois in Urbana-Champaign (1996–97).

TEN ARQUITECTOS TEAM

The following people have worked for TEN Arquitectos:

PARTNERS

Enrique Norten
Bernardo Gómez-Pimienta

CURRENT TEAM

Catalina Aristizábal
Rosana Castañón
Gabriel Diaz
Aarón Hernández
Carlos López
Claudia Marquina
Sergio Núñez
Francisco Pardo
Miguel Rios
Hugo Sánchez
Mark Seligson

Bárbara Escamilla
(secretary)

FORMER TEAM MEMBERS

Christianne Abel
Raúl Acevedo
Miquel Adriá
Juan Carlos Aguilar
Ramón Álvarez
Julio Amézcua
Axel Arañó
Bernardo Barona
Agustín Berenguer
Laurence Bertoux
Ernesto Betancourt
Kenneth Bostock
Jaime Cabezas
Antonio Cangas
Blanca Castañeda
José Manuel Castillo
José Ángel Centurión
Rafael Chi
Jean Michel Colonnier
Ana María Cruz
Francisco Cruz
Jesús Alfredo Domínguez
Valeria Espinosa
Gustavo Espitia
Daniel Esquenazi
Marco Fantini
Fernando Fernández
Jorge Flores
Sergio Gallardo
Hector L. Gámiz
Eli Garcilazo
Raúl Garduño
Hussein Garzón

Rebeca Golden
Miguel Ángel González
Margarita Goyzueta
Daniel Granados
Molly J. Grimmett
Francisco Gutiérrez
Armando Hashimoto
Chantal Hayaux Du Tilly
Jimena Hernández
Elena Hurtado
Mónica Jiménez
Sergio Juárez
Miguel Ángel Junco
Daniel Kafka
Yolanda Kelly
Sarit Kreff
Rodrigo Laguna
Javier Macías
Margarita Macías
Ana Martínez
Ileana Martínez
Jorge Martínez
Erick Monroy
Luis Montalvo
Luis Muciño
Sergio Nuñez
Carlos Ordóñez
Mario Padilla
Antonio Pavón
Alejandra Peña
Hector Pérez
Jorge Luis Pérez
(former partner)

Manuel Portillo
Xavier Presas
Marco Antonio Pulido
Rogelio Rendón
Sergio Reyes
Héctor Rico
Gabriel Rodríguez
Sergio Rodríguez
Arturo Rojas
Elizabeth Rosales
Carlos Ruiz de Chávez
Gerardo Sánchez
Hugo Sánchez
Ana Santillana
Roberto Sheinberg
Jorge Soto
Juan Carlos Tello
Roberto Toledo
Sigfrido Ulloa
Carlos Valdez
Oscar Vargas
Fernando Vázquez
Alejandro de la Vega
Cesar Villareal
Carlos Yáñez
María Carmen Zeballos
Úrsula Zulch

María García
(secretary)
Magdalena Maldonado
(administration)

List of Projects

Dates refer to year of commission. Dates following individual entries in parentheses refer to year of construction.

1997

EL CAMINO REAL HERITAGE CENTER
Holmes-Sabatini and Associates, associate
architects. Socorro, New Mexico. In progress.

ADDAMS HALL AND FINE ARTS BUILDINGS
University of Pennsylvania. Philadelphia,
Pennsylvania. Renovation and additions.
In progress.

COPILCO HOUSING
Coyoacán, Mexico City. In progress.

SOCIAL SCIENCES BUILDING
Arizona State University. Tempe, Arizona.
In progress.

COLLEGE OF ART AND ARCHITECTURE
University of Michigan. Ann Arbor, Michigan.
Renovation and additions. In progress.

JAGUAR DEALERSHIP
Gilberto Borja, associate architect. Santa Fe,
Mexico City. Invited competition. First place.

1996

HOTEL LAMARTINE
Polanco, Mexico City. Invited competition.
First place. In progress.

NURSING AND BIOMEDICAL SCIENCES BUILDING
University of Texas Health Science Center at
Houston. Houston, Texas. Invited competition.
Second place. Unbuilt.

HOUSE RR
Desierto de los Leones, Mexico City. In progress.

HOUSE RO
La Jolla, California. In progress.

1995

TELEVISA PRODUCTION BUILDING
Chapultepec, Mexico City. Unbuilt.

MUSEUM OF SCIENCES
Chapultepec Park, Mexico City. In progress.

1994

LA ANGOSTURA HOUSING
Bosques de las Lomas, Mexico City. Unbuilt.

SANTA FE PAVILION
Santa Fe, Mexico City. Unbuilt.

HOUSE LE
Condesa, Mexico City (1995).

1993

HOUSE X
Lomas de Chapultepec, Mexico City (1995).

TELEVISA SERVICES BUILDING
Chapultepec, Mexico City (1995).

NATIONAL SCHOOL OF THEATER
Churubusco, Mexico City (1994).

INSURGENTES THEATER
San José Insurgentes, Mexico City (1995).
Renovation and additions.

LC PHOTOGRAPHY STUDIO
San Miguel Chapultepec, Mexico City.
Unbuilt.

OLA AZTECA (STADIUM AND CONCERT HALL)
Santa Úrsula, Mexico City. Unbuilt.

FINSA OFFICES
Paseo de la Reforma, Mexico City.

ALPA OFFICES
Granjas México, Mexico City.

1992

NATIONAL CENTER FOR THE ARTS
Churubusco, Mexico City. Invited competition.
First-place tie. Unbuilt.

JAFRA OFFICES AND DISTRIBUTION CENTER
Santa Úrsula, Mexico City. Unbuilt.

LOCATEL-08 OFFICE BUILDING
Del Valle, Mexico City. Unbuilt.

TELEVISA DINING HALL
San Ángel, Mexico City (1993).

IBERO-OLMECA UNIVERSITY
Villahermosa, Tabasco. Invited competition.
Second place. Unbuilt.

SEISMIC RESEARCH INSTITUTE
Coyoacán, Mexico City. Unbuilt.

1991

MODA IN-CASA (FURNITURE STORE AND MAIN OFFICES)
Lomas de Chapultepec, Mexico City (1993).
Invited competition. First place.

CENTRO AUTOMOTRIZ
Santa Fe, Mexico City. Unbuilt.

BOSTON CHILDREN'S MUSEUM
Boston, Massachusetts. Invited competition.
Second place. Unbuilt.

GRUPO ARGÜELLES INDUSTRIAL PARK
Iztapalapa, Mexico City (1992).
WORKERS HOUSING BRASIL 75
INFONAVIT. Mexico City (1992).
WORKERS HOUSING LA VIGA 95
INFONAVIT. Mexico City. Unbuilt.
WORKERS HOUSING GONZÁLEZ ORTEGA 7
INFONAVIT. Mexico City. Unbuilt.
HOUSE P
Lomas de Chapultepec, Mexico City (1993).
TEPITO 2000 (COMMERCIAL CENTER AND URBAN PROJECT)
Mexico City. Unbuilt.
LA TEJERÍA HOUSING
Villahermosa, Tabasco. Unbuilt.
PARQUE ESPAÑA (URBAN PROJECT)
Condesa, Mexico City. Unbuilt.
C.I.M. HIGH SCHOOL CAFETERIA
Lomas de Vistahermosa, Mexico City. Unbuilt.

1990
ALLIANCE FRANÇAISE
Lindavista, Mexico City (1992).
Invited competition. First place.
HOUSE O
Bosques de las Lomas, Mexico City (1991).
APARTMENT G
Lomas de Chapultepec, Mexico City (1991).
SPACE OFFICES
Polanco, Mexico City (1990).
AVITEC OFFICES
Juárez, Mexico City (1991).
CHILDREN'S MUSEUM
Bosque de Chapultepec, Mexico City.
Invited competition. Second place. Unbuilt.
F. FWD. CITI COMMERCIAL CENTER
Acapulco, Guerrero. Unbuilt.

1989
DUOMO (FURNITURE STORE)
Polanco, Mexico City (1990).
PECANINS ART GALLERY
Roma, Mexico City (1989).
HOUSES N AND R
Cruz de Misión, Valle de Bravo (1990).

HOUSE AND WORKSHOP H
Otumba, Valle de Bravo (1993).
APARTMENT G
Lomas de Chapultepec, Mexico City (1990).
TARANGO PARK (URBAN AND LANDSCAPE DESIGN)
Lomas de Tarango, Mexico City (1989).
LOS OLIVOS PARK
Tláhuac, Mexico City. Unbuilt.

1988
LIGHTING CENTER (SHOWROOM AND OFFICES)
Colonia Roma, Mexico City (1989).
Renovation and additions.
HOUSE NO
Cruz de Misión, Valle de Bravo (1989).
ALEXANDER VON HUMBOLDT HIGH SCHOOL
Lomas Verdes, Estado de México.
Invited competition. Fifth place. Unbuilt.

1987
HOUSE M
La Herradura, Estado de México (1988).
APARTMENT A
Polanco, Mexico City (1988).

1986
CLOROX INDUSTRIAL PLANT AND OFFICES
Tlanepantla, Estado de México (1986).
APARTMENT W
Lomas de Chapultepec, Mexico City (1987).
TEPITO (URBAN REDEVELOPMENT PROJECT)
Mexico City. Unbuilt.

1985
HOUSE S
Bosques de las Lomas, Mexico City (1986).
APARTMENT ME
Miami, Florida (1985).
APARTMENT LN
Lomas de Chapultepec, Mexico City (1985).
CONVENTION CENTER
Valle de Bravo, Estado de México. Unbuilt.
SAN CARLOS HORSE RANCH
Zumpango, Hidalgo. Unbuilt.
GUADIANA PARK
Durango, Durango. Unbuilt.

Bibliography

Writings by Enrique Norten

"Inmaterial Architecture." In *Anybody*, edited by Cynthia Davidson, 190–95. Cambridge, Mass.: MIT Press, 1997.

"Particular in the Global." *Architecture California* (Los Angeles) 17, no. 1 (May 1995): 74–75.

"A Personal View." *I/A Network* (Washington, D.C.) (fall 1993).

"Encuentros en la ciudad." *Arquitectura* (Mexico City) 4 (winter 1992): 27.

"Luz, color, espacio: la arquitectura de Carlos Jiménez." *Arquitectura* (Mexico City) 5 (spring 1992): 54–57.

"Cinco casas: la ciudad en la suburbia." *Construcción Mexicana* (Mexico City) 274 (July 1982): 24–32.

Books, Monographs, and Exhibition Catalogs

Acévez, Luis Mariano, and Guillermo Eguiarte. "Viviendas para obreros." In *Anuario de arquitectura 1992–1993,* edited by Adriana Léon, 82–87. Mexico City: Arquitectura, 1993.

Adriá, Miquel. "Escuela Nacional de Teatro, TEN Arquitectos." In *México—90s: una arquitectura contemporánea,* 126–33. Barcelona: Editorial Gustavo Gili, 1996.

——. "Escuela Nacional de Teatro." In *Anuario 1994,* 62–69. Mexico City: Arquitectura, 1995.

Alva Martínez, Ernesto, ed. *IV Bienal Mexicana de Arquitectura, 1995–1996.* Mexico City: Colegio de Arquitectos de la República Mexicana, 1996.

——. *Tercera Bienal de Arquitectura Mexicana, 1994.* Mexico City: Colegio de Arquitectos de la República Mexicana, 1994.

Álvarez Noguere, José Rogelio, ed. *Seis años de arquitectura en México: 1988–1994.* Mexico City: Universidad Nacional Autónoma de México, 1994.

American Institute of Architects. *Highly Adaptive Strategies for New Professional Realities: Young Architects Forum.* San Antonio, Tex.: American Institute of Architects, 1992.

Arquitectura Mexicana: Primera Bienal. Mexico City: Federación de Arquitectos de la República Mexicana, 1990.

Asensio, Francisco. "Houses by the Sea." In *Adecuación moderna a la tradición,* 210–17. Architectural Houses, vol. 3. Barcelona: Ed. Atrium, 1992.

Bienal de Arquitectura de Buenos Aires, 1993. Buenos Aires: CAYC, 1993.

Broid, Isaac. "Casa 'R,' Valle de Bravo." In *Anuario de Arquitectura: México 1991,* 56–59. Mexico City: Arquitectura, 1992.

Canadian Centre for Architecture. *The Architect's Sketchbook: Current Practice.* Montreal: Canadian Centre for Architecture, 1992.

Carter, Brian, ed. *The Work of TEN Arquitectos.* Ann Arbor: Michigan Architecture Press, 1997.

Collins, Karen, and Pollyana Nordstrand. *Myth and Modernism in Mexican Architecture.* Fullerton, Calif.: California State University Press, 1994.

Contemporary Architectural Drawings. San Francisco: Promenade Editions, 1991.

Creación en movimiento: becarios 1991–1992. Mexico City: FONCA, 1993.

Creadores en movimiento: generación de becarios 1990–1991. Mexico City: FONCA, 1992.

"Enrique Norten: reflexiones de quince años." *Enlace* (Mexico City) 2, no. 9 (September 1992): 16–23.

Gally, Gerardo, ed. *Enrique Norten: arquitecto.* Foreword by Carlos González Lobo and Lebbeus Woods. Monografías, vol. 1. Mexico City: Editorial Concepto, 1987.

González Gortázar, Fernando. *La arquitectura mexicana del siglo XX.* Mexico City: Consejo Nacional Para La Cultura y Las Artes, 1994.

Hollein, Hans. "Sensori del futuro: l'architetto come sismógrafo." In *Scuola di Teatro, Cita de Messico,* 216–17. Milan: Electa, 1996.

Noelle, Louise. *Contactos: en el límite de la arquitectura y la escultura.* Mexico City: BANAMEX, 1994.

Noelle, Louise, and Carlos Tejeda. *Catálogo-guía de arquitectura contemporánea, Ciudad de México.* Mexico City: Fondo Cultural Banamex, 1993.

Norten. San José de Costa Rica: Colegio de Arquitectos de Costa Rica, 1995.

RICALDE, Humberto. "Taller de Enrique Norten y Asociados." In *Arquitectura mexicana: 10 obras—anuario 1990,* 22–25. Houston: Westmore and Co., 1990.

SASLAVSKY, Ricardo, ed. *Reseña de arquitectura mexicana 1992.* Mexico City: Enlace, 1993.

SERGIO, Ronay. *Fast Forward City.* Mexico City: Space, 1991.

SOLÁ-MORALES, Ignasi, and Xavier Costa. "TEN Arquitectos: Workers Housing." In *Present and Futures: Architecture in Cities,* 130–31. Barcelona: Collegi d'Arquitectes de Catalunya, 1996.

TOCA, Antonio, and Carlos Vejar. "Tienda de muebles." In *II reseña de arquitectura mexicana,* 256–59. Mexico City: Fundación Casa del Arquitecto, 1995.

Urbanismo III—Internacional: Cidades do futuro. São Paulo: Grupo Panorama, 1987.

Via NY. Mexico City: Galería Sloan-Racotta, 1986.

WOODS, Lebbeus. *TEN Arquitectos.* Catálogos de Arquitectura. Barcelona: Editorial Gustavo Gili, 1995.

ZABLUDOVSKY, Abraham. *Taller de Enrique Norten y Asociados.* Mexico City: Galería Pecanins, 1989.

JOURNALS, MAGAZINES, AND NEWSPAPERS

1997

"Casa LE en Ciudad de Méjico." *Diseño Interior* (Madrid) 58 (February 1997): 94–99.

"Centro de Arte Dramático." *Enlace* (Mexico City) 7, no. 3 (March 1997): 40–45.

HO, Cathy. "Workers Housing, Mexico City, 1992." *Design Book Review* (San Francisco) 37–38 (winter 1996–97): 59.

MACINNES, Katherine. "Media Friendly." *World Architecture* (London) 53 (February 1997): 50–51.

"Merecido premio." *Reforma* (Mexico City), June 2, 1997, suplemento etremuros, 12.

"Oficinas A: serenidad para un ámbito de trabajo." *Diseño Interior* (Madrid) 61 (May 1997): 104–7.

PASSAMANO, Chris. "Input Sought on $35 Million State-of-the-Art Building." *Arizona State University Press* (Tempe), September 15, 1997, 1.

"TELEVISA Mixed-Use Building." *GA Document* (Tokyo) 50 (April 1997): 104–11.

"TEN Arquitectos: House RR." *GA Document* (Tokyo) 52 (April 1997): 112–23.

"TEN Arquitectos: House Z, House LE." *GA Houses* (Tokyo) 51 (March 1997): 116–39.

VITTA, Maurizio. "Cemento, acciaio e legno: House LE, Mexico City." *L'Arca* (Milan) 112 (February 1997): 76–79.

1996

ADRIÁ, Miquel. "Tendencias en la casa contemporánea mexicana." *Origina* (Mexico City) 4, no. 41 (August 1996): 24–27.

BOSSI, Laura. "TEN Arquitectos." *Domus* (Milan) 783 (June 1996): 111–12.

DORIGATI, Remo. "Un'icona televisiva in Mexico City." *L'Arca* (Milan) 108 (October 1996): 58–63.

"Enrique Norten: Casa LE." *Quaderns d'arquitectura i urbanisme* (Barcelona) 213 (fall 1996): 134–37.

GÁMEZ, Silvia Isabel. "Busca la arquitectura punto de intersección." *El Universal* (Mexico City), June 28, 1996, sec. C, 1.

GIOVANNINI, Joseph. "Mexican Modern." *Architecture* (Washington, D.C.) 85, no. 12 (December 1996): 64–69.

INGERSOLL, Richard. "Norten." *Lotus* (Milan) 91 (November 1996): 50–59.

MACMASTERS, Merry. "La arquitectura apunta a condiciones menos concretas, más abiertas." *La Jornada* (Mexico City), July 6, 1996, sección cultura, 27.

MATSUYA, Keiko. "Mexican Design." *Wind* (Tokyo) 34 (spring 1996): 24–25.

"Museum of Natural History." *Architecture* (Washington, D.C.) 85, no. 5 (May 1996): 154–57.

NOELLE, Louise. "Network." *Tostem View* (Tokyo) 58 (March 1996): 14.

———. "Ondas anodizadas: edificio de servicios para TELEVISA." *Arquitectura Viva* (Madrid) 47 (March–April 1996): 86–89.

PALACIOS GOYA, Cynthia. "En la arquitectura, no hay niños prodigio." *El Nacional* (Mexico City), August 23, 1996, sección cultura, 41.

PEARSON, Clifford A. "School of Dramatic Arts." *Architectural Record* (New York) 184, no. 3 (March 1996): 90.

RAN, Ami. "When Form Follows Geometry, Form Does Not Necessarily Follow Function." *Architecture of Israel* (Tel Aviv) 24 (January 1996): 42–56.

"TEN Arquitectos." *Korean Architects* (Seoul) 143 (July 1996): 88–173.

WEATHERSBY, William, Jr. "National Center of the Arts: Mexico City." *Theatre Crafts International* (New York), May 1996, 34–35.

——. "Teatro de los Insurgentes: Mexico City." *Theatre Crafts International* (New York), May 1996, 44–47.

1995

BALINT, Juliana. "Transparent." *Moebel + Decoration Wohnen* (Leinfelden-Echterdingen, Germany), 1995, 68–71.

CASCIANI, Stefano. "Cittá del Messico: l'arte della vendita." *Abitare* (Milan) 336 (January 1995): 114–17.

CROMBIE, Edward. "Dramatic Art." *The Architectural Review* (London) 1178 (April 1995): 59–62.

"Enrique Norten—Drama Center." *GA Document* (Tokyo) 44 (August 1995): 64–73.

FERNÁNDEZ-GALIANO, Luis. "Imágenes del tránsito: Enrique Norten y el libre comercio de las formas." *Arquitectura Viva* (Madrid) 40 (January–February 1995): 32–39.

GONZÁLEZ Pozo, Alberto. "Mexiko baut." *Deutsche-bauzeitung* (Stuttgart) 129 (February 1995): 66–71.

GÜEMES, César. "La arquitectura contemporánea ha eliminado el concepto de estilo." *El Financiero* (Mexico City), April 26, 1995, sección cultural, 57.

"House LE." *GA Houses* (Tokyo) 45 (March 1995): 152–53.

"House O." *GA Houses* (Tokyo) 46 (June 1995): 52–63.

INGERSOLL, Richard. "Global Technics." *Architecture* (Washington, D.C.) 84, no. 9 (September 1995): 78–83.

——. "Mex-Tec Transmission." *Architecture* (Washington, D.C.) 84, no. 12 (December 1995): 76–83.

——. "Scuola Nazionale di Teatro a Cittá del Messico." *Casabella* (Milan) 623 (May 1995): 60–66.

LARRAÑAGA, Enrique. "Casa Ortiz." *Economía Hoy* (Caracas), September 16, 1995, sección arquitectura hoy, 5.

MERELES GRAS, Louise. "La obra y su autor." *Novedades* (Mexico City), June 23, 1995, sec. C, 12.

PAVARINI, Stefano. "Variazioni sul tema." *L'Arca* (Milan) 93 (May 1995): 60–71.

RÍOS, Oscar. "Andamiajes para palacios de madrugada." *Diseño* (Santiago) 30 (March–April 1995): 66–71.

RUIZ, Blanca. "Está 'Hecho en México' y listo para exportar." *Reforma* (Mexico City), September 22, 1995, sección cultura, 14D.

SICUSO, Francisco. "Experimento espacial." *La Prensa* (Buenos Aires), March 2, 1995, sección arquitectura.

"Taller de Enrique Norten Arquitectos." *Arquitectura* (Mexico City) 14 (October 1995): 32–45.

"TELEVISA Mixed-Use Building." In "American Architecture 1995—Forty-Second Annual *Progressive Architecture* Awards." *Progressive Architecture* (Stamford, Conn.) 75, no. 1 (January 1995): 112.

"Two Projects by Enrique Norten." *Korean Architects* (Seoul) 127 (March 1995): 48–65.

1994

"Architecture: What's Going Up in Mexico." *Los Angeles Times,* November 1994, Orange County edition, sec. F, 1–2.

BALINT, Juliana. "Enrique Norten in Messico: continuitá con sorpresa." *Abitare* (Milan) 331 (July–August 1994): 74–79.

——. "Transparent." *Moebel + Decoration Wohnen* (Leinfelden-Echterdingen, Germany), August 1994, 26–31.

"Enrique Norten—Recent Work." *Korean Architects* (Seoul) 123 (November 1994): 14–29.

Fernández-Shaw, Enrique. "Lo que hacemos y no vemos." *Economía Hoy* (Caracas), March 12, 1994, sección arquitectura, 2–3.

González Silva, Matiana. "Un gran conjunto para crear." *Siglo 21* (Guadalajara), December 3-4, 1994, suplemento casa abierta, 4–5.

Gudiño, Bernardo. "Arquitectura como metalenguaje." *Educación Artística* (Mexico City) 2, no. 7 (November–December 1994): 3–10.

Kunkel, Susana. "Enrique Norten." *Ovaciones* (Mexico City), October 29, 1994, suplemento espacios.

López Padilla, Gustavo. "A la hora de comer." *Arquitectura* (Mexico City) 11 (summer 1994): 28–37.

Massuh, Lilia Y. "Diversidade e tradiciao." *Arquitectura e Urbanismo* (São Paulo) 56 (November 1994).

Mereles Gras, Louise. "Convirtiendo lo abstracto en realidad." *Entorno Inmobiliario* (Mexico City) 2, no. 12 (November–December 1994): 50–54.

———. "Rompiendo esquemas." *Entorno Inmobiliario* (Mexico City) 2, no. 7 (January–February 1994): 48–52.

Moorhead, Gerald. "Under Cabled Arches." *Architectural Record* (New York) 182, no. 11 (November 1994): 68–73.

Porter, Luis. "Enrique Norten." *Reforma* (Mexico City). May 26, 1994.

Ryan, Raymund. "Life in the Gap." *Architectural Review* (London) 1169 (July 1994): 62–64.

Waisman, Marina. "Tradición de vecindario: viviendas sociales, Ciudad de México." *Arquitectura y Vivienda* (Madrid) 48 (July–August 1994): 90–93.

Walsh, Daniella. "Building Modern Mexico." *Orange County Register*, November 25, 1994, arts section, 78.

1993

Betsky, Aaron. "Modernist Courtyard." *Architectural Record* (New York) 181, no. 7 (July 1993): 86–89.

Eguiarte, Guillermo. "Entre actualité et originalité." *L'Architecture d'aujourd'hui* (Paris) 288 (September 1993): 72–79.

"Enrique Norten: PP House, Z House." *GA Houses* (Tokyo) 37 (April 1993): 110–13.

Frachon, Pierre. "Atelier TEN." *L'Architecture d'aujourd'hui* (Paris) 288 (September 1993): 80–87.

Krämer, Karl H.. "Französisches Institut in Mexiko-Stadt, Mexiko." *Architecktur + Wettbewerbe* (Stuttgart) 156 (December 1993): 28.

"La arquitectura como arte." *Memoria de Papel* (Mexico City) 3, no. 6 (June 1993): 75–80.

López Padilla, Gustavo. "Aires de cambio." *Memoria de Papel* (Mexico City) 3, no. 6 (June 1993): 82–87.

Maceda, Elda. "Redescubrir el lenguaje de la arquitectura." *El Universal* (Mexico City), November 26, 1993.

MacMasters, Mary. "Enrique Norten, premio latinoamericano de arquitectura." *El Nacional* (Mexico City), November 26, 1993.

Mereles Gras, Louise. "Convirtiendo lo abstracto en realidad." *Novedades* (Mexico City), December 17, 1993.

Noelle, Louise. "Casas de México." *Premier* (Mexico City), spring 1993, 60–70.

Oxandeberru, Roura. "La Alianza Francesa–Centro Cultural Lindavista." *Arquitectura* (Mexico City) 8 (April 1993): 34–41.

1992

Emerich, Luis Carlos. "Post y neomexicanidad" *Casa Vogue* (Mexico City), June 1992, 134–39.

Flores, Luis Vicente. "Interiores." *Arquitectura* (Mexico City) 5 (spring 1992): 17–33.

Lavin, Sylvia. "Modernidad festiva: la Casa Ortiz de Enrique Norten." In "El cuerpo doméstico." *Arquitectura Viva* (Madrid) 23 (March–April 1992): 44–47.

———. "Ortiz House." *Architecture + Urbanism* (Tokyo) 264 (September 1992): 60–67.

Longoria, Rafael. "After Barragán: Redefining Mexican Modernism." *Texas Architect* (Austin) 42, no. 5 (September–October 1992): 40–47.

MacCall, Peter. "Norten: Mexican Modernism." *AIA Journal* (Washington, D.C.), October 1992.

"Parque de los olivos." *Arquitectura* (Mexico City) 4 (winter 1992): 54–57.

"Parque Tarango." *Arquitectura* (Mexico City) 4 (winter 1992): 32–35.

PRÖHL, Undine, and Horst Rasch. "Viel Haus auf Viel zu Kleinem Grundstück." *Häuser* (Hamburg), April 1992, 98–99, 110–13.

RAN, Ami. "Sketchbooks: What Comes Out of Them." In "The State of the Art." *Architecture of Israel* (Herzlia) 13 (August 1992): 64–76.

STEIN, Karen D. "Site Lines." In "Record Houses 1991." *Architectural Record* (New York) 180, no. 4 (April 1992): 90–95.

"Tepito 2000." *Arquitectura* (Mexico City) 6 (summer 1992): 51–53.

TORRES ALPUCHE DE LANKOWSKY, María. "Zeitgenösische Architektur in Mexiko." *Bauwelt* (Berlin) 35 (September 1992): 1958–79.

WARMAN, Eddy. "Arquitecto Enrique Norten, creador de ambientes." *Cablevisión* (Mexico City), August 1992, 84.

———. "Distinción." *El Universal* (Mexico City), August 4, 1992, sección sociales, 1.

1991

CHAO BARONA, Enrique. "Obra del mes: un prisma de luces." *Obras* (Mexico City), April 1991, 10–22.

KALACH, Alberto. "Museo del Niño—tres propuestas." *Arquitectura* (Mexico City) 1 (spring 1991): 7–15.

LÓPEZ, Gustavo. "Tradición y modernidad." *México en el Diseño* (Mexico City) 1, no. 2 (February–March 1991): 8–10.

LÓPEZ ALVERDE, Alberto. "Línea 8, Ciudad de México: propuestas alternativas." *Arquitectura* (Mexico City) 2 (summer 1991): 56–60.

PERRELLA, Stephen. "Enrique Norten: Recent Work." *Newsline* (New York) 4, no. 2 (November–December 1991): 4.

PRÖHL, Undine, and Horst Rasch. "Punktsieg über die Denkmal Schützer." *Häuser* (Hamburg), February 1991, 96–97.

1990

"Expondo as entranhas." *Design e Interiores* (São Paulo) 3, no. 21 (November 1990): 97–99.

FREIMAN, Ziva. "Enrique Norten." In "Young Architects." *Progressive Architecture* (Stamford, Conn.) 71, no. 7 (July 1990): 87.

GASKIE, Margaret. "Bringing Light." *Architectural Record* (New York) 2 (February 1990): 84–87.

MUTLOW, John. "Mexican Architecture—New Directions." *LA Architect* (Los Angeles), January 1990.

WHITESON, Leon. "Mexican Designers Embrace the New." *Los Angeles Times*, February 1, 1990.

1989

LÓPEZ, Gustavo. "Nueva Generación." *Excelsior* (Mexico City), November 26, 1989.

"30/30." *Interiors* (New York), September 1989.

1987

"E tempo de reconsiderar a modernidade." *A + U* (São Paulo), November 1987.

1986

EMERICH, Luis Carlos. "Los 'cuartos exteriores' del arquitecto Enrique Norten." *Vogue* (Mexico City) 7, no. 70 (March 1986): 114.

MACNAIR, Andrew. "Enrique Norten." *Architectures* (New York), August 1986.

1985

HERNÁNDEZ, Maüe. "Enrique Norten y el lengüaje moderno de la arquitectura." *Activa* (Mexico City) X-23 (November 1985): 50.

1984

"14 proyectos mexicanos para la Ópera de la Bastilla." *Arquitectura y Sociedad* (Mexico City) 37, no. 29 (October 1984): 13–42.

1983

SOMORROSTRO, Carlos. "Cinco Casas." *Arquitecto* (Mexico City) 24 (June 1983).

"'The Peak' participación mexicana." *Construcción Mexicana* (Mexico City) 286 (July 1983): 37–48.

1982

"El Jardín de las Memorias." *Croquis* (Universidad Iberoamericana, Mexico City) 6 (May 1982).

"Reflexiones sobre la arquitectura en el ocaso del siglo XX." In "Post-modernismo." *Construcción Mexicana* (Mexico City) 275 (August 1982): 27–40.